PRAISE POEMS

PRAISE POEMS

THE KATHERINE WHITE COLLECTION

SEATTLE ART MUSEUM

Cover: Mother and child figure, Zaire, Luba, 19th-20th century (cat. no. 16)

Frontispiece: Staff (Eshu), Bamgboye of Odo-Owa, Nigeria, Ekiti Yoruba, 20th century (cat. no. 25)

Catalogue coordinator: Suzanne Kotz
Editor: Lorna Price
Design: Ed Marquand

Photo credits: © Ralph Marshall—cat. nos. 1, 2, 3, 5, 6, 7, 8, 9, 10, 11, 12, 13, 14, 15, 16, 19 (detail), 21, 23, 24, 27, 28, 31, 32, 33, 34, 35, 37 (detail), 38, 41, 42, 43, 44, 46, 47, 48, 49, 51, 52, 53.
Paul Macapia—cover, cat. nos. 4, 17, 18, 19, 20, 22, 25, 26, 29, 30, 36, 37, 39, 40, 45, 50.

Printed and bound in Japan by Nissha Printing Company, Ltd., Kyoto.

Library of Congress Cataloging in Publication Data
Main entry under title:

Praise poems.

Published in conjunction with a traveling exhibition of objects from the collection.
Bibliography: p.
1. Sculpture, African—Africa, West—Exhibitions.
2. Sculpture, Primitive—Africa, West—Exhibitions.
3. White, Katherine—Art collections—Exhibitions.
4. Sculpture—Private collections—Washington (State)—
Seattle—Exhibitions. I. Seattle Art Museum.
NB1098.P73 1984   730'.0966'074   83-51840
ISBN 0-932216-15-3 (paper)
ISBN 0-932216-16-1 (cloth)

This book is published in conjunction with the exhibition, *Praise Poems: The Katherine White Collection*, organized by the Seattle Art Museum.

Major funding for the exhibition and catalogue has been provided by the National Endowment for the Arts, PONCHO (Patrons of Northwest Civic, Cultural, and Charitable Organizations), and the Mellon Foundation. In Seattle, the exhibition and its programs are supported by grants from the American Express Foundation and Foster & Marshall, a division of Shearson/ American Express; the Washington Commission for the Humanities; and the Seattle Trust Guest Artists Program.

TABLE OF CONTENTS

FOREWORD

African praise poems traditionally herald persons of merit and mark their memory for a form of renown. Here we offer homage to African art and to the collector Katherine Coryton White. The exhibition calls to assembly fifty-three heroic works to serve as outriding ambassadors for a collection of over 2,000 objects. The catalogue announces in poetic form the presence of those pieces specially favored by Mrs. White, while for each work a scholarly detail of origin and use is given.

When a place receives the name of its discoverer, or an object is associated with a collector, it is a historical accident. It is, however, not an accident when powerful works, drawn together by a consuming act of devotion, seem stronger together than apart. We pay homage, therefore, to the works themselves by acknowledging the impulse that revealed them to us.

The Katherine White bequest and a second extraordinary gift that made it possible stimulated a series of changes that have given a new character to the activities of the Seattle Art Museum. A curatorial department of African, American, and Oceanic native art, a growing international scholarly network, and substantial new programmatic services to the Seattle community are all witness to the authority these works of African art exercise upon us.

The number of those who have supported the collection and have helped settle it in Seattle is large. I should like to give special thanks, however, to Bagley and Virginia Wright who, with Charles Cowles, introduced Mrs. White to Seattle and for almost a decade made her welcome in this community. Thanks are due also to Mr. Wright and, particularly, Kenneth Fisher, who negotiated the unique circumstances under which the museum was able to meet the requirements of Mrs. White's intent and later gift bequest.

Enthusiasm for the works in the collection is also evident in the generous financial support received from numerous sources. Grants from Mr. and Mrs. John H. Hauberg and the National Endowment for the Arts have made possible the process of housing, cataloguing, and conserving the collection. The National Endowment for the Arts, PONCHO (Patrons of Northwest Civic, Cultural, and Charitable Organizations), and the Mellon Foundation have all generously supported research, publication, and circulation of this exhibition. Additional funding for the exhibition and programs in Seattle has been provided by the American Express Foundation and Foster & Marshall, the Washington Commission for the Humanities, and the Seattle Trust Guest Artists Program. To them we are very deeply grateful.

The research and scholarly substance of the catalogue is the result of the expert guidance and contributions of Dr. Roy Sieber, Dr. Robert Farris Thompson, and Pamela McClusky, the associate curator for ethnic art at this museum. Recognizing that full documentation of the collection has just begun, the effort of these scholars will serve as inspiration for those that follow. I should also like to thank Suzanne Kotz, head of publications; Paul Macapia and Ralph Marshall, photographers; Bonnie Pitman-Gelles, associate director for programs; Lorna Price, editor; Ed Marquand, designer; Norman Skougstad, curatorial assistant; and Paula Thurman, publications assistant, for their contributions.

Arnold Jolles
Director

"My house is a solid volume of
space saturated with art. Like a
presence thick as concrete are the
humming and whining and sing-
ing of pictures, sculpture: stand-
ing room only.

"They are magic and art both.
An African mask, a New Guinea
totem, an Indian club are all
immersed so deeply in the life of
their contexts that they are inex-
tricable. They are as close to their
native landscapes as grass, as
wind...They do not stand there
insisting they are beautiful.
Theirs is a kind of efficiency...
working as silently as a clock gear,
and as discreetly...As I admire
them, propaganda does not
intrude. They are intersections of
form and time. So am I...I bring
myself to a work of art with all the
known and unknown qualities of
myself. What it is in terms of who
I want to be, what I am in terms
of what I will be after a lifetime of
watching. I choose carefully..."

Katherine Coryton White

KATHERINE C. WHITE: TWO TRIBUTES

I Remember Kat

Alfonso Reyes, the great Mexican poet, once remarked that for certain persons time makes a strong dosage of oblivion *(una fuerte dosis del olvido)*. In contrast, the brilliant spirit rises above the rapidly blurring, rapidly fading images of ordinary time. Katherine Coryton White is clearly a time-resistant spirit, blessed with energy and grace.

I first saw her, from afar, at a symposium at Columbia in the spring of 1965. Fresh from a doctoral campaign, I was slightly dazed and disassociated. Nevertheless, I clearly have the image of her sweeping in, admirers and fellow collectors handsomely attendant. Then one year later in Dakar, during the First World Festival of Black Art, Roy Sieber introduced us. I was immediately impressed by her wit, her drive, her boundless energy, the glee with which she threw herself into the building of one of the major collections of the visual traditions of Africa.

In 1968 she invited me to an audience at the Cleveland Museum of Art on the occasion of the first exhibition of her collection. At this point I became aware of the total context of her life, devoted to art and matters of creative impress and equilibration. High-spirited as a professional athlete—we raced a freight-train in her car for the sky-blue hell of it—and very competently read, she was a master of her field in every sense. "What did you think of that concert of modern music?" someone asked her. "A chrome-plated wave" was her response. Continuously alive. I never dreamt one day I would be pulled into the very center of this creative vortex.

But I was. In the fall of 1971 came a long-distance call from Kat, to Hamden from Westwood Village, asking me to write a catalogue for the second exhibition of her collection of African visual art. I flew almost immediately to Cameroon and searched the southwest quadrant of that mighty nation for traditional dances in which to allow particular objects in her collection— by then burgeoning—to step forth in full indigenous glory. It was a pleasure to work with her, knowing that films of Basinjom, videotapes of Egungun, sessions with traditional women and men of words and erudition would be greeted by that special nonstop enthusiasm that marked her mode of realist being. She was a master teller of tales of voyage, e.g., of a horse that wandered into a restaurant in Bobo-Dioulasso ("He was old, very old, had two teeth, and I fed him sandwiches which he artfully worked back to the working portion of his mouth"), of suffering pompous academic fools ("When in the presence of egomaniacs one's proper role is wallpaper, however tiresome that might be"), or explaining why X refused to marry Y, the cruel industrialist ("She could have never been certain at a dinner party that she wasn't seating her husband next to someone he had just ruined!").

It would take Cimino himself, or Joan Didion, to do justice to the pace and texture of her style of life, the way she could instill drama and joy in so ordinary an act as packing for a foreign trip ("warm clothes, cool clothes"—the phrase instantly encoding a flight to the tropics, followed by a zigzag north). In a world dreary with indecisiveness, she knew what fun was and how to share it. From the dulcet problem of how to fit in motion contexts key monuments from her collection, and then what to do with the many *other* pieces, too, arose a decision to work on gesture and on stance as well as dance per se. And that portion of my encounter with Kat and art changed indelibly the way I work, and led eventually to an exhibition on gesture and iconology in Kongo.

After that joyous intense experience, the making of *African Art in Motion*, Kat and I went our separate ways. She helped Roy Sieber find treasure for his superb exhibition of African furniture and household objects, just as she had earlier lent a knowing hand to the photographic campaigns and search periods of the Sieber textile exhibition. I had always hoped to work with her again, in the making of an exhibition called *Faces of the Goddesses and Gods: Shrines and Altars of the Black Atlantic World*. But I know that when I complete this exhibition, some three years hence, her powerful spirit will be there, a wind between the lights, a mind behind the persons, an eternal suppliant before the moral grandeur of Africa and her visual traditions.

Robert Farris Thompson

Katherine C. White: A Personal Reminiscence

I first met Kat White in the mid-1960s. It was, if I recall correctly, at a conference at Columbia University. We sat next to each other, making *sotto voce* asides about the papers. It seems, in retrospect, that much of our friendship consisted of asides. We discussed ideas and objects: brilliant ideas and superb objects as well as objects of doubtful authenticity (which made her "nervous") or pieces of doubtful quality (which left her "underwhelmed") or fakes (which made her furious).

Soon after we met we began co-curating an exhibition of African textiles and personal decoration for the Museum of Modern Art in New York. That is not quite accurate; we began with plans for a show of all forms of African decorative art, but as the results of Kat's tremendous job of photographing American collections began to accumulate, we discovered that there existed a mine of unexhibited and unpublished material, enough to cause us to revise our original plan. We decided to focus that show on the human body as carrier.

Before the Museum of Modern Art show was even installed, we had decided that all the ignored areas from that exhibition should become the basis for a second show. This time the compound would be the focus for a show of furniture and household objects. That exhibition did materialize under the aegis of the American Federation of Arts. Again Kat made her photographic rounds; again the richness of the collections amazed us.

The working photographs—really slides—were from the first planned to become a research tool of longer and larger significance than the time-bound exhibitions; indeed, one set of the slides (more than 3,500 of them) is available to researchers and students at Indiana University. The workaday nature of the archival slides, often taken under less than ideal settings in museum storerooms or the homes of collectors, somewhat masks the fact that Kat was an excellent photographer who produced an impressive portfolio of color images of eroded, timeworn surfaces and objects.

With the exception of a delightful little Kongo doctor's whistle which she had purchased in France in 1949, Kat did not begin her serious and extensive collection of African art until eleven years later. It eventually included sculptures, utilitarian objects, jewelry, and textiles; nothing African of aesthetic merit escaped her view or evaded her grasp.

She loved the pieces in her collection once they had passed her tough and exhaustive scrutiny. Although she trusted her own eye, she succumbed at times to the opinions of others. She regretted that she gave up a favorite object because it had been doubted by an expert; she came finally to believe she was right, the expert wrong. Another time she hid deep in a closet a mask that others had called a crude, atypical example and probably a fake; years later, she was delighted to discover that field research conducted after she had purchased it showed it to be

a genuine example of an unpublished style. If a piece failed to pass muster, or if later she became unsure of its authenticity, she was neither sentimental nor outraged. Instead, without regret, it quietly and quickly disappeared from the collection.

She was omnivorous as a collector of things: Italian marble eggs, driftwood, shells, mineralogical crystals, prints, paintings, anything that appealed. But she never confused what she found personally inviting with the place of that object in the larger scheme of things. Yet she loved some objects even when she was perfectly aware that they were not masterpieces. She would point out the major pieces in the collection with pride and considerable understanding. Then, with a wry smile, she would say, "But look at this delicious (charming, witty, extraordinary, outrageous) piece," and chuckle with delight at her flouting of the pompous. Thus she was audacious at times, buying an outrageous work, one that was not popular with collectors nor central to the academically fashionable scheme of African art; witness her early interest in textiles, jewelry, furniture. I recall that in Dakar we came upon a small female figure, possibly Baga in origin, dressed in European clothing—red dress, shoes. In those days (the mid-1960s), a serious collector did not acquire such "recent," "influenced," "westernized" figures. Afterwards she would insist, with mock exasperation, that I had "forced" her to get it, but then she would say, with her characteristic deep giggle, that she adored it. She insisted that it be included in the Cleveland catalogue written by William Fagg.

When she began collecting, she made it a high priority to get to know museums, collectors, and scholars. Among the many she respected and, indeed, loved were William Fagg and Margo Plass. She traveled in Africa with them. She listened, argued, and learned. She told me several times that she gained much from Arnold Rubin's lectures at UCLA; she rarely failed to attend meetings and symposia. Yet she never considered herself more than an amateur, deferring to the experts, the academics. She might fight tooth and nail about the quality of a piece and be far more than casually knowledgeable about it, but she left scholarship to scholars. At the same time, she was realistic about them, sharply aware and respectful of their strengths and equally aware of sham, weakness, or puffery.

She was a connoisseur in the very real and dictionary sense of a discriminating critic. Indeed, in her pursuit of African art she was a dilettante in the admirable, original eighteenth-century meaning of that term: an inspired, wise, and dedicated amateur.

Roy Sieber

Fig. 1. Katherine White's home, Seattle, 1979. Photo by Paul Macapia.

INTRODUCTION

Katherine White presided over a compression chamber of African creativity. Everyone who entered her home was visually assaulted by hundreds of assertive faces and expressive figures that occupied every wall and tabletop, filled every room and closet (fig. 1). To ensure the unnerving extravagance of it all, Mrs. White might hand the visitor a figure for the purpose of exploring its surface, or offer a sloping stool to sit upon. Then, to test one's expertise, she might require an opinion of an Oceanic sculpture set in the middle of a herd of carved African animals. It was an eclectic profusion, conspicuously confusing, as befitted the tastes of a private collector.

In a museum, the intimacy and profusion of the collector's private cabinet is replaced by an insistence on the visual challenge offered by each individual work of art. The galleries inevitably rely on understatement. To amend their austerity, this catalogue attempts to recount the experience of viewing these works of art in an African setting. It begins with art of a public nature and ends with that usually only seen in strict secrecy. Proceeding from the everyday to the extraordinary, the viewer is guided through many different African "galleries" or viewing situations—public arenas, household courtyards, shrines, royal courts, public performances, and restricted performances. Illustrations of these "galleries," selected from slides taken by Katherine White in Africa, may bring the viewer closer to seeing how specific works of art fit

specific African contexts.

Suggesting the hierarchy of African "galleries" is one way of enhancing Western awareness of the importance that many African artworks once held in their own milieux. In viewing works familiar to Western cultural orientations, such as a Roman equestrian statue or a Gothic madonna, we easily supply the historical and connotative background through common awareness of the art, its origins, and its context; a familiar image, or first-hand experience, rounds out the museum setting. Visual images of a large, lively public square in Italy, or the somber interior of a tall cathedral, establish references for Western sculpture and what it once meant to the culture of which it was a part. This tour of several African "galleries" reveals visual and experiential references not readily available to many viewers of African art.

African sculpture is often thought of as coming from a village, a setting commonly misconceived as being not only uncomplicated, but one in which sculpture is virtually ubiquitous. But neither assumption is the case. In African villages, open displays of sculpture per se are actually few, although ornamentation of surfaces is commonplace. Certain landmarks seen by everyone, such as polychrome posts or modelled mud walls, are added to buildings to form exteriors of distinction and artistically proclaim the status of the owner (figs. 2, 3). A visitor being led into courtyards and compounds of particular households would see cer-

Fig. 2. Yoruba veranda, Illesha, Nigeria, 1964.

tain implements that might draw attention because of their artistry. A bowl (cat. no. 1) might be handed over, to open a time of discussion. Stools (cat. nos. 3, 4) whose supports had been turned into caryatid sculptures would become the obvious seats for leaders. A set of harps (cat. no. 6) in the hands of a travelling musician could add a visual facet to his profession. Yet in the arena of daily public life in African settings, sculpture is not seen as a permeating presence, but more as a punctuating device.

Usually set aside from everyday village life, African shrines establish a special and separate arena for viewing sculpture. Shrines vary widely in structure; some are large, open, community gathering points, while others are small, private consultation chambers meant only for individual use. However defined, they establish a sanctuary where an

3

Fig. 3. House exterior, Sha, Nigeria, 1964.

profusion of paraphernalia for worship. Bowls full of offerings, old bottles, rattles, shells, mirrors, candles, and an endless host of sacred ingredients might be spread out in clustered arrays around the sculpture, all barely visible in muted light. The complex interaction of media and iconography signifies an arena requiring respect and guidance to comprehend. In the midst of such an impressive assembly, the focus is frequently a human image, calm and composed, taking its place in a surround of spiritual intensity.

An altar is usually attendant to the shrine sculpture; it furnishes a repository for the offerings and sacrifices meant to open channels of communication between the visitor and the deity. To establish soothing relations, a person might offer cool water, milk, chalk, honey, cereal, or yam. To ignite forceful relations, wine, beer, gin, hot pepper, or chicken blood could be sprayed or poured onto the altar. Many members of a community frequently make their way into shrines to observe the imposing display and work with the image of the shrine in finding solutions to a variety of community ills. In the exhibition are sculptures meant to be visited in shrine complexes devoted to healing, enhancing fertility, divining the future, systems of justice, and controlling warfare and aggression (cat. nos. 8-13).

Private and often personal shrines are set aside for individual use. Small consultation chambers featuring a work of art provide a

image sits in an aura of sacred presence. Sculptures kept in these special houses often depict paragons of human character—men and women who are poised, dignified, and devoted to ideal behavior. Not gods, but as morally and spiritually distinguished as humans can be, they provide role models and contact with divinities to whom the shrine may be dedicated.

Outdoor shrines are often open to the community and can be subtly constituted (fig. 4). A significant road junction, a cluster of rock formations, or a grove of trees are places where the potential for

a spirit's appearance is considered to be strong. Images placed there receive libations meant to entice a deity to reside in the sculpted form. Durable terracotta images (cat. no. 14) exposed to rain and sun once stood in outdoor shrines to honor leaders of the past. Successive generations of adherents could visit them in the dense foliage of their forest shrines.

Indoor shrines are often highly complicated displays (figs. 5, 6). Crossing the threshold into the shrine might require permission of a priest or priestess. Inside, the sculpture would be revealed amid a place for a person to withdraw, in order to concentrate on problems and relationships with spiritual concerns. When incorporated into a domestic setting, a shrine figure might be seen daily and treated like a human companion, fed when attentive and reprimanded when negligent. Nearly all the figures presented in private shrines in this exhibition are female (cat. nos. 16, 17, 19, 21, 22). Young women and mothers are frequently portrayed in African art that is kept in personal or family chambers. The female usually becomes a touchstone for thoughts about conception, the need for nourishment, family welfare, and continuity of lineage.

Royal artwork is seen periodically. When presented, it is not quietly contemplated, but part of a profuse and ostentatious display that emphasizes the power and wealth of the ruler (fig. 7). Rather than the studied interaction that occurs in a shrine, a viewer sees the art from a distance, as the monarch passes by or initiates ceremonies involving sculptural symbols that distinguish his status. Works from the Kom and Benin kingdoms are included in this selection of royal art (cat. nos. 28-30). They were once insignia of

Fig. 4. Dogon marker, Miango, Mali, 1968.

Fig. 5. Interior of a Yoruba shrine, Ibadan, Nigeria, 1964.

Fig. 6. Chief Ovienrioba's shrine, Benin City, Nigeria, 1964.

two prominent African rulers—a sixteenth century Oba of Benin and a nineteenth century Fon of Kom. The Oba paraded annually outside the confines of a magnificent palace through a city surrounded by three miles of walls, wide streets, and rows of organized residential areas. Massive crowds gathered to see the Oba's display of pageantry. Similarly, the Fon of Kom dressed in resplendent regalia, and was encircled by a panoply of royal sculpture, leopard pelts, tusks, and royal cloth when he appeared in public. Most of the year royal leaders were relatively, if not completely, inaccessible to ordinary mortals. Public glimpses of the royal court were rare and fleeting, but customary. Through these elaborate appearances, the ruler was able to display works of art that exemplified the splendor of his reign and maintained his distance from commoners.

Performances are the artistic arena most removed from the museum context. Whereas many figural sculptures can be appreciated in the stable environment provided by a museum, masks are created for kinetic display at differing times of the day and night, in events filled with dance, song, music, drama, lavish costumery, and audience participation (figs. 8, 9). Only those who stay in a village throughout a performance season are privileged to experience the full effect of a masquerade. Months of preparation activate the community, each person contributing to the overall effect of

Fig. 7. Oba Akenzua II in procession, Benin City, Nigeria, 1964. Photo by Werner Forman.

Fig. 8. Performance, Bamenda, Cameroon, 1966.

6

a performance. Considerable excitement builds as ordinary duties give way to a time of symbolic actions. When the mask finally appears, it is immersed in a complicated orchestration of dynamic theater.

Turning the wooden mask into a full masquerade requires many steps. A carved face or helmet is the bare beginning. It must be carefully painted or oiled to present a fresh surface. Then the performer dresses, sometimes in a costume concealing his identity and creating an entirely new one. Costumes are not only colorful, but can be musical, as when bells, rattles, anklets, and bracelets form a percussive accent to the ensemble. So dressed, a masked performer is transformed into a complete character with its own songs, choreography, and dramatic intent. Masks in this exhibition portray humans, animals, and composite spirits which were seen in public performances. Several were involved in initiations, the teaching of proper codes of behavior, and the passing-on of cultural knowledge (cat nos. 39-41). Others performed at funerals, a time of catharsis and celebration when maskers honor the dead and encourage their transition into spirit realms (cat. nos. 33, 34). Some human masks performed to review and occasionally parody members of a community on a regular basis (cat. nos. 35-38).

While many masks perform during predictable seasons with full community support, there are also masks of less than public appeal. Women and children are often forbidden to see restricted performances; such masks are usually the last artwork to be revealed to a visitor in an African context. Instead of being greeted with jubilation, these masks appear as a sign that tensions have arisen and that serious dimensions of society are to be addressed. They are called upon to confront disorders which threaten to undermine a society's self-confidence: lawbreakers, signs of excess, disease, ugliness, and the presence of malevolent spirits.

To perform this duty, the masks are deliberately odious or mysterious. Menacing faces with extreme distortions are worn with concealing costumes that allow no sign of human form to show (cat. nos. 47, 51). Others appropriate emblems from aggressive animal avatars— fur, feathers, teeth, claws, horns, and hair (cat. nos. 48, 53). Indeed, many masquerades of this kind derive more from animal characterizations than from human identities (cat. nos. 45, 50). The maskers do not sing, but utter inhuman sounds and disguise their voices with growls and whistles. They do not dance, but lurch through villages with irregular movements. Throughout their performance, they portray an unearthly personality, often an awesome, beastial force to be avoided but heeded. Through this masked anonymity, they may deliver punishments and accusations to those who have broken social rules.

Fig. 9. Performance, Fada N'Gurma, Upper Volta, 1969.

Fig. 10. Bamunka village, Cameroon, 1966.

Each of the fifty-three artworks in this exhibition once occupied a unique arena for viewing. A radically generalized attempt to describe a few African "galleries" is offered to enable the viewer to begin to visualize an environment more compelling than the museum gallery, more complex than the seeming simplicities of village life. In addition, this exercise, through a tiny sampling of illustration, also reveals that Katherine White accumulated not just works of art, but a good measure of documentation in hopes of keeping alive our ongoing dialogue with African artistry.

Pamela McClusky
Associate Curator of Ethnic Art

1. Container *(opon)*
Nigeria
Northern Yoruba, 20th century
Wood, pigment
L. 57.5 cm. (22 5/8")
81.17.618

"There's a homogeneous ease here. It's a pattern pool. A man's torso slides into a box, the box in turn finds itself on four legs with a sudden tail. The horse is stylized in lizards and geometric lozenges. Articulated too is the arrogance of the exercise. With a look of ineffable assurance, there is high humor on the horse's face. The visual fix slides into place like an oiled bolt."—KCW

A horse and rider are consolidated in one container. The rider holds the reins high, creating a convenient handle for lifting the lid in order to expose the container's contents. Kola nuts, offered to guests as a sign of hospitality, were probably stored within. Visitors would split the nuts and chew them for a dose of bitter caffeine. The breaking of these nuts often constituted a pact of loyalty and friendship.

In counterpoise to this generosity, the horseman is also a well-equipped warrior. He may carry the intention of a proverb into visual form, "Peaceful words bring a kola nut... but hard words bring an arrow from the quiver" (Delano, 1966, p. 107). In anticipation of the latter circumstance, he holds a curved sword in his right hand and a large sword with decorated scabbard under his left arm. His jutting chin also signals his protective readiness. Extensive decorations copy the style of northern leather and fabric trappings over the body of the horse. Green stain on the trappings adds a final touch to this unusual *opon*.

10

2. Veranda post *(opo)*
Nigeria
Yoruba, Adechina School of Owo-
Eye, 20th century
Wood, pigment
H. 194 cm. (76 3/8")
81.17.626

In Yoruba cities, sculptured poles and posts were landmarks identifying buildings of consequence. Entrances to special homes and the interior courtyards of palaces and shrines were lined with figural poles. Carved sentinels offered a public statement of the status or sacred nature of the space within.

Most poles were actually structural supports for the roofs of verandas common to Yoruba architecture. They had to be carved from a hardwood to sustain weight and resist insect attacks. A series might be commissioned to adorn several sections of a prominent building. Their number declared the artistic preference of the owner and the qualities of character he favored.

Here, an equestrian holds tight reins on a horse with a high-pommeled saddle. Horses were scarce possessions among the Yoruba and in the past had usually been owned by important leaders. As a further sign of status and authority, this figure holds a flywhisk that curves over his right shoulder. The horse is caparisoned with reins, saddlecloth, bridle, and stirrups, all depicted in detail.

Two women stand beneath the chieftainly horseman. They hold their bare breasts to greet the visitor. While offering affection, they also signify modesty and devotion to their public position. Eyes downcast, they attest to the inward power of endurance and patience *(iroju)* appropriate to worship a deity or support a ruler whose presence they announce.

During the early part of this century, the carving school of Adechina centered in Owo-Eye answered a constant demand for such artistry. A walk into many neighboring towns would have been highlighted by signposts designating where prominent and sacred personalities had met.

12

"Dignity is compressed into a column with total confidence. Every compromise is well handled. Dark and light females form the base. ... Next, the horse is foreshortened and politely squeezed in. Then the supreme rider. ... He presides over all the shadowed faces with a guarding expression and huge effervescent eyes."

—KCW

A geometric organization of anatomy is evident in every angle of this Chokwe caryatid. The shoulders, torso, hands, and feet have all been distilled into flat rectangles, while the arms and legs form swelling, opposing curves. This contrast of full muscles and flat planes fulfills a Chokwe aesthetic preference for dynamism in the human form.

Round stools *(shiki)* were insignias of the Chokwe ruler known as the lord of the land *(mwanagana)*. Such rulers commissioned professional carvers *(songi)* to surround their court with artistry. Staffs, pipes, cups, chairs, and figures were among the emblems they carved for the Chokwe aristocracy. *Shiki* may not have been conceived until the late nineteenth century, when the Chokwe expanded their territory and came in contact with the prolific stool precedents carved by their Luba and Pende neighbors. On the top of this stool, *songi* carvers added the gleam of brass studs obtained through trade as a sign of status.

Two sets of markings on the caryatid's torso reveal her sex. Straight ridges known as *kapula* incisions cut at puberty rites and *mahenga* cicatrices on the abdomen are both female traits. This woman crouches beneath the seat with her hands to her head in a gesture of lamentation. In sitting upon her image, a Chokwe ruler may have symbolically acknowledged his need for female support and assistance.

3. Stool *(shiki)*
Kwilu-Kasai area, Zaire
Chokwe, 19th–20th century
Wood, brass studs
H. 33.7 cm. (13 1/4")
81.17.914

"There is more than one kind of figure here and no one place in which to know her. From the back there is inhuman geometry in beautifully manicured spaces. From the side suddenly all those shapes slide out, becoming arms, legs, a hairdo.... From balanced squares emerge voluptuous curves with convincing suavity.... See also how the legs billow out like a sail full of wind and resolve to thin paperlike feet. How the head rushes and elongates only to close into a tightly fit face."—KCW

4. Stool *(kihona)*
Zaire
Luba (Hemba style),
19th-20th century
Wood
H. 50.8 cm. (20″)
81.17.876

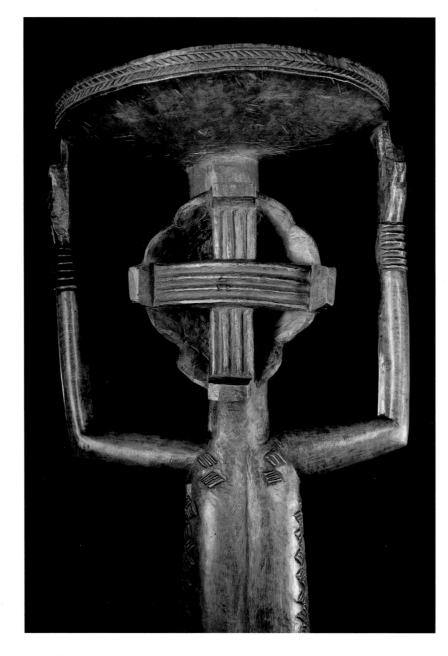

Two types of Luba body art are highlighted on this stool's caryatid. Her torso is textured by an intricate series of raised patterns, representing the welted skin of Luba scarification. Cicatrices like this were formed by light incisions into which the juices of particular plants were rubbed, causing the skin to contract and leave a raised welt. Such patterning made women's bodies exciting to see as well as to touch. Many Luba stools recorded the designs of this art very meticulously, and some women were said to have journeyed for days to consult a stool and affirm the correct alignment of certain markings.

This caryatid's hairstyle depicts another pervasive aspect of Luba fashion. It often took an entire day or more to complete one coiffure, with husband and wife each preparing the other's hair. Oil, clay, and cane frameworks were sometimes utilized to create sculptural styles that could last two to three months. Here the woman's head has been shaved from ear to ear to emphasize a high domed forehead, while most of her hair has been gathered in the back into four braids in a crosslike formation. So embellished, this caryatid properly represents a woman of high rank.

16

Sculptural stools *(kihona)* were the prerogative of family heads, as well as of chiefs and kings. A leader sat upon it in formal hearings to demonstrate authority as he dispensed justice or presided over disputes. Since most Luba clan rulers traced their right to rule through their female relatives, the stool could also serve as a metaphor of the feminine support of their exalted position.

Several virtuoso Luba carvers have been identified. The artist who carved this stool is tentatively credited with the creation of another stool, a figurated bowl, and a bow rest. In each example of this anonymous artist's work, the broad forehead, closed eyes, tightly held lips, and stomach patterning are similar. The anatomical adjustments in the two stools are nearly identical. Legs form a diminutive adjunct to the base; the arms rise at angles to the torso and become a tripod of vertical support along with the head and its columnar extension. This stool was collected in 1916 in the field by a Belgian military officer, Roger Castiau, who may also have collected a stool purchased by the University Museum at the University of Pennsylvania in 1919.

5. Stool *(ko)*
Mbanga, Cameroon
Mambila, 19th-20th century
Wood
W. 46.4 cm. (18 1/4″)
81.17.724

If a Mambila woman had difficulty during childbirth, this stool was brought out for her to sit upon. The supportive caryatids then became her witnesses, hearing confessions of any guilt or other problems which might be contributing to her condition. Both sides of the stool bear upholding figures whose bodies are adapted to this task. One side depicts a male and female figure splayed and squatting with their hands over their heads. The other depicts a row of intertwined bodies with hands held over their stomachs. A woman in labor would sit on the stool and grasp the sides. The Mambila believed that the stool would encourage her to admit any offenses and thereby release whatever might be contributing to her anxiety, and thus the difficulty of the birth.

Delivery stools belonged to the patriarchs of a cluster of compounds. This example was discovered out in the open near a sacred grove located in the center of a compound.

19

6. Pair of male and female harps
Zaire
Ngbaka, 20th century
Wood, skin, fiber
H. 68 and 66 cm. (26 3/4″, 26″)
81.17.882.1,.2

Anatomy is stretched and condensed to suit the form of these humanoid harps. Long curving necks hold five pegs which once supported strings of varying length and pitch. The strings terminated in the ovoid, hide-covered bellies that served as resonating chambers. Legs carved in the round and slightly flexed enable the instruments to balance as free-standing sculptures and imply a dancing step.

Harps were not actually played to encourage dance, but accompanied the songs and narrative stories and fables recited by professional musi-cians. Recordings of harp lutes played by solo male singers from areas of Central Africa document this musical and narrative tradition.

Among the Ngbaka, many folk tales and legends revolved around a main protagonist named Seto. An informant has also stated that Seto is the name assigned to their harps (Laurenty, 1960, p. 182). Thus, in his performance, the musician visually and orally illustrated the Ngbaka's sense of Seto as an all-encompassing character.

Through legends Seto reveals himself to be "a jolly fellow, lazy and careless, fond of women, a bit of a boaster and joker, playing tricks on others when he can, but without meanness, fond of laughing and dancing, which he taught to men" (Vergiat, 1951, p. 58). Seto is often accompanied by his wife Nabo, which might explain the reason for the clearly female gender of one of this pair. Together they are consid-ered cultural founders whose protec-tion and assistance are sought in preserving health, increasing fertil-ity, providing harvests, and assuring success in hunting.

20

7. Horse and rider
Mali
Dogon, late 19th century
Wood
H. 36.5 cm. (14 3/8″)
81.17.46

"A horse is supreme extravagance.
No demeaning fate awaits him—
no plow, no chores. He is an
adjunct to display, a carrier of
superiority. Look at the authority
of that rein, the permanence and
the subjugating will.

"Tall, self-bemused, the man
inhales the intoxicating air know-
ing that earthbound, he is only
ridiculous."—KCW

Obvious and obscure references
tend to merge in Dogon art. Here
the riding of a horse is an immedi-
ate sign of distinction. Horses in
West Africa were not beasts of bur-
den. The liabilities of maintaining
them in the African landscape were
various and quite costly. Only
empires, kingdoms, and a few indi-
viduals of considerable means were
able to import and outfit horses.
When a man on horseback is
sculpted, he usually portrays a
leader, aristocrat, or warrior.

Dogon equestrians are often
referred to as *hogons*, the priests
and political leaders of Dogon cul-
ture. The *hogon* is a ritual authority
for his village, insuring a daily
observance of Dogon cosmology.
Accounts of a mythical nature lead
to other less obvious interpretations.
One of many possible myths implied
by this sculpture is that of a found-
ing father of Dogon existence. The
first blacksmith, when living in the
heavenly workshops, assembled ani-
mals, grains, and technological
knowledge in an ark. His last neces-
sity was a piece of the sun, which he
stole in the form of white hot iron
and glowing embers. He then leaped
onto the ark and hurtled down to
earth on a rainbow. When he fell to
earth, his sinuous limbs were broken
at the elbows and knees. His newly
jointed arms and legs made it possi-
ble for him to work, whereupon he
took the horse from the ark and set
out in search of land to cultivate.

In accordance with this myth, the
horseman's body is sculpted as a
series of geometric units broken at
sharp angles. As the ark followed the
rainbow to earth, it travelled in a
zig-zag pattern, which may account
for the incised lines on the horse
and rider. This appears to be a her-
maphroditic depiction combining
female breasts with a penis; the orig-
inal Dogon were thought to have
both male and female souls. With
his head tilted back and his horse
forging ahead, this sculpture may be
an austere reminder of the founding
blacksmith setting out on his path to
establish culture.

Myths also suggest that sculp-
tures were carved just at the time a
death occurred, to provide the spirit
of the deceased with an object to
reside in. The *hogon* had jurisdic-
tion over the shrines where the fig-
ures were kept. Actual patterns
of use have not been securely
documented.

This perplexing physique defies exact identification. A head is evident, since round eyes are set into a solid sphere. Beneath it a quizzical face of three projections descends to portray a nose, flanked either by a set of distended ears or a pendulant coiffure. An extremely attenuated body follows. The columnar neck and tapering torso form a central axis that extends two-thirds of the figure's total height. Irregular ribbonlike arms twist around the torso in jagged segments. Short notched legs bluntly repeat the rippling of the arms. As the torso twists in a direction opposite to the head and neck, a formal tension actively engages the viewer. The Mumuye thereby create a figure whose planes and volumes are set in undulating opposition.

Thousands of Mumuye figures were functional artworks until the late 1960s. During the era of civil disorder in Nigeria, a large number of carved figures appeared on the

international art market without documentation. As a consequence, the individual use and meaning of the figures in a Mumuye context may never be clarified. General roles have been described for Mumuye figural traditions. The earliest source identifies such figures as resting places for the spirits of deceased parents. Later research reports that figures presided over the entrance to a rainmaker's compound and wandered through the domestic area, serving as guardians. Occasionally the figure acted as an oracle, which was activated by coating its face with plant sap; it was then asked to expose wrongdoers. Figures could also become witnesses to oaths, were embraced to determine truth and falsehood during trials, and played a part in healing rituals performed by healers and diviners. This figure might have served in any one of these diverse yet often overlapping roles.

An equestrian and his snake-charming wife form a rare sculptural couple from Yorubaland. They were presented as a pair to two anthropologists in 1958 by the king (Alafin) of Oyo. Subsequently separated for many years, the couple was reunited in 1981 to sustain their unusual relationship. He is a mounted military officer physically prepared for battle. A long braid of hair *(asiso)* emerges at the top of his head and curves down the back of it. *Asiso* are grown to cover incisions made to receive apotropaic substances that are applied to render warriors fearless. Rectangular talismanic leather pads around his neck afford additional protection. A hole in his right hand probably once held a spear or lance *(oko)*, the usual weapon of the Oyo cavalry. With this armor of potent inner preparations and weapon, he was outfitted for one of the many battles waged on behalf of the Oyo domination and later Yoruba civil wars of the nineteenth century.

At his side, the wife wears two vivid clues to her identity—a snake biting its own tail and an iron bracelet. Only one type of woman is known to appear with a snake hung around her neck like a chain—an *ijala* chanter or Iya Ologun. *Ijala* chanters carry toothless pythons *(ejomonamona)* as insignia of their role as verbal artists. They perform for mortals, especially warriors and hunters, but ultimately chant for Ogun, the god of war and iron. *Ijala* chants are lengthy verses of praise for distinguished warriors and hunters of the past, often combining poetry and episodes of history. Ogun is said to be appeased by hearing talented chanters and will protect warriors and hunters when he hears them.

9. Equestrian and female figures
Oshogbo-Edi area, Nigeria
Yoruba, 19th century
Wood, camwood powder, indigo dye, coconut-shell beads, iron, leather
H. 66 cm. and 65.4 cm.
(26", 25 3/4")
81.17.606; Margaret E. Fuller Purchase Fund 82.124

Part of an *ijala* chant could almost describe this couple:

> Wawa is the hunter in charge of the world,
> Olugbu-ele is the hunter in charge of heaven;
> They control hunting in the forests,
> Osoosi is Ogun's only wife,
> She helped make him the finest hunter
> But could not hunt herself....
> (Williams, 1974, p. 299)

The couple coalesces not only in form but in purpose. The two re-create the alliance of a warrior or hunter with an *ijala* chanter who once supported him with verbal tribute. Their sculptural duality may have served as a focal point for an Ogun shrine. Ogun is a beneficent but dangerous deity who is credited with a major technological achievement, the discovery of iron. He thus enabled tools to be made, which made life easier, but at the same time made possible the creation of instruments of battle. In the Ogun cult, the role of violence in human experience is considered, as is the fact that men can invent technology capable of destroying culture. These sculptures possibly stood as monuments of commitment to Ogun's two-sided discovery.

Rarely is Ogun represented by figural sculpture; usually his altars are designated by iron implements or stones. Although this couple's unique iconography contains many of Ogun's attributes, this interpretation is not the first, and may not be the last to be applied to them. When this pair was collected in the 1950s, the Alafin of Oyo stated that the couple had been housed at Old Oyo, a capital which fell during a Fulani invasion in 1830. He identified the horseman as Alajogun and the female as Aje, "the witch."

27

10. Shrine figure *(ivri)*
Nigeria
Urhobo, prior to 1925
Wood, pigment, nails, sacrificial
deposits
H. 92 cm. (36 1/4″)
81.17.532

"This is an expert with a glut of
thick force. Ugly, crusted like a
poisoned skin, the *ivri* growls,
pulls his fangs apart, shows a cave
of disgust and anger. Such rage
beyond containment.... How can
anything so hideous be art? How
can lethal fury be art? ... It's a
progression out of the dungeon.
First man is there, normal. Then,
birds in flight and finally the gen-
tlest of all creatures, the elephant,
bringing wisdom weightlessly."
—KCW

The *ivri* is an image deemed capable of devouring human aggression. Its hybrid form is well suited for that purpose, as large incisors open wide to dominate an ambiguous body. From the monstrous base, a human triad with united arms is surmounted by birds and a creature standing on human heads.

The Urhobo rationale for the *ivri* reveals the intent of its configuration. An *ivri* was carved for individual or collective use when hostility arose. If a man became persistently troublesome and argumentative, unwilling to adjust or share, an *ivri* would be commissioned on his behalf. His *ivri* then acted as a personality corrective, demanding that he recognize the need to contain his antagonistic instincts. Regular offerings of food were deposited in this *ivri*'s cavernous mouth to satisfy its hunger for aggression. When properly acknowledged, the *ivri* was content and insured that the owner's antagonism was subdued.

A small portion of an Urhobo praise poem for the *ivri* collected in 1971 reveals its potential if fed:

> Protect the world
> One sits firmly
> So that you can protect the world
> As you protect both younger and
>   older children
> Warning: being worried by hunger
>   brings vexation
> Hunger makes you say what you do
>   not understand
> Warning: this is the *cola* for him.
>   (Foss, 1976, p. 287)

In other situations, the *ivri* might take on active roles. A warrior needing to channel his energies for battle or the capture of enemies might consult his *ivri* for assistance. Community groups needing protection from slave raiders or warfare might also keep an *ivri* as a guardian force. A forgetful person whose possessions were stolen or misplaced could ask the *ivri* to help him regain what had been lost.

An *ivri* nearly identical to this one was recorded in use in a small antechamber at the rear of a town meeting hall in 1959. There it received offerings of yams, chicken and dog blood, gin, and kola nuts provided by members of the Ughienvwe lineage. This example is coated with a crusty layer of residue from similar treatment. Spots of red and white pigment also coat the surface of the *ivri* and cover the eyes of each figure. The red is derived from camwood and is suggestive of fertile elements, while the white is kaolin clay from the riverbeds between water and land, and thereby indicative of religious purity.

The composite *ivri* centaur addresses the positive and negative, the personal and collective force that aggression can take. It provides the Urhobo with a metaphorical way of controlling its effect on human personalities.

29

11. Oath-taking and healing image
(nkondi)
Zaire
Kongo, 19th century
Wood, iron, fiber, beads
H. 79.4 cm. (31 1/4″)
81.17.836

"Danger gathers. Nails, hammered iron made to penetrate by violence with twine, earth, chain, hair, beads, gum, bone, the crust of dusty air. It's like a poisonous mane, festering, prodding like antennae. Lethal. Each addition is an episode of pain and revenge which hangs with accumulated malice.... The face waits for an utterance, the tongue hovers, the nails seethe, the eyes like a vacant chrysalis behind their glass insist on a frozen focus."—KCW

Nail figures tend to be typecast as fetishes executing episodes of hostility and revenge. Revised interpretations now credit the *nkondi* with a wide range of roles including the ability to end disputes, divine guilt, and dispense justice. Among the many powers ascribed to *nkondi* sculptures are the curing of epilepsy, relief of stomachaches, and protection against theft and the malice of antisocial witchcraft.

The massive mane of nails which engulfs this figure's torso signifies more than merely evil intent. Each one was driven into the *nkondi* at the conclusion of a legal debate, healing session, or treaty. Hundreds of nails attest to the hundreds of Kongo citizens who consulted with the *nkondi* to seek his disciplined judgment.

At the *nkondi*'s side, a *nganga* or "morality engineer" usually was present to advise clients how properly to address the *nkondi*. He might select the type of nail (hand-forged or European import) and recommend a further action of commitment. Two disputing parties who had finally reached an agreement or resolution might be required to meet, feast together, tie a piece of hair or string to the nail, kiss it, and swear on it before pounding it into the *nkondi*. From then on, the *nkondi*, alerted to their pact, has the authority to cause harm if the pact is not honored. This *nkondi* harbors a variety of irregular iron and manufactured nails, as well as tied-on beads and string to distinguish the requests of each client.

Beneath the nails this figure is in prime muscular condition and stands in a posture called *pakala*, hands on hips, arms akimbo. His stance is that of one who is ready, alert, and waiting to render complicated decisions concerning the dilemmas brought to his attention. *Nkondi* figures were usually kept in a house of their own at some distance from the village they served.

30

"The wood is rigid as iron. Rain hasn't rotted it, nor have centuries of insects gnawed their caves with accustomed ease. Ekom is dense and refuses change. He is a monument, a time-marker, pacing an entire generation. Each clan had its own tall crowd of Ekom figures representing nine, twelve, sometimes fourteen steps into the past. The tall dim body rises in a procession of slow parentheses: the strong belly of a king, the flywhisk of government, the narrow manicured beard of a patriarch. The face is cool, the crack only deepens his concentration."—KCW

When a male Oron elder died, a hardwood was chosen to carve his representative image, since memories of him were meant to last. Emblems to signify his prominence were incorporated into the carving. Here a flaring hat and flywhisk indicate a man of prestige, perhaps an important chief. He also wears an elongated, plaited beard, an Oron fashion of previous generations. His body is conceived in the Oron manner, as a series of segmented and stacked anatomical regions. When carved and dedicated by the living elders of the village, the *ekpu* figure became the tangible locus for the deceased. Through it, a recently deceased elder could continue to have an influence on his descendants.

Rows of columnar *ekpu* figures were stored in a shrine building *(obio)*. Twice annually the figures were visited and honored with sacrifices of food and drink. Elders would preside as the *ekpu* were approached for aid in making fertile the visitors' farms and families.

Ekpu carving was an active art form for nearly 200 years until the twentieth century (c. 1750-1900). After carving ceased, many figures succumbed to the dense tangle of forest growth in decaying outdoor shrines. By the 1940s a survey revealed over 1000 *ekpu* in Oron territory. This accumulation became the rationale for a temporary museum with over 600 figures, which opened in 1967. That was also the year the Nigerian civil war erupted, resulting in the evacuation of the museum. Before the war ended many *ekpu* met tragic ends. By 1978 the Oron Museum had opened once again to display enduring rows of majestic *ekpu* monuments.

12. Figure *(ekpu)*
Calabar Province, Nigeria
Oron, c. 18th-19th century
Wood
H. 97.8 cm. (38 1/2″)
81.17.515

33

13. Reliquary figure *(eyima)*
Gabon
Fang, 19th-20th century
Wood
H. 51.1 cm. (20 1/8″)
81.17.783

Fang reliquary figures issue a visual warning. This figure guarded the *bieri*, a cylindrical bark box containing the sacred relics of Fang families. Lashed to the box with vines, the *eyima* was kept in a small hut outside the village to defend the *bieri* from any antisocial or rival elements who might, by trying to harm it, unsettle family welfare. Women and those not initiated into the *bieri* cult were strictly forbidden to see the *bieri* and this attendant figure. The relics of *bieri* so protected were primarily collections of craniums selected from illustrious men and women of the past.

Watching over this profound segment of lineage history and genealogy, the *eyima* image concentrates on his obligation. The relic and statue together evoked the idea of the deceased members of the clan who were accessible when needed. Before undertaking any change, whether a voyage, marriage, war, or placement of a new village, the head of the family might consult the *bieri* to ask for aid and protection.

Bieri were removed from their seclusion for initiations, divination, and curing procedures. On all these occasions the chiefs of the lineage enforced caution and extensive purification before the relics could be seen. For initiation the neophyte chewed trance-inducing herbs to render him capable of entering into relations with the dead. Officals rubbed the statue and bones with oil and watched over the young men who passed into comas filled with visions brought on by the *bieri*'s presence. Music and dance, including a manipulation of the statues behind a cloth screen, completed the experience.

A remarkable tension is inherent in the statue's form. The face implies a remote concentration on the potential threat of unseen forces. Simultaneously, the muscles strain with strength. Severe passivity and potential energy are held in balance.

14. Funerary head
Ghana
Akan, mid-19th century
Terracotta
H. 24.8 cm. (9 3/4")
81.17.322

"African clay is roughshod stuff, never inert. Grit, mica, sand, and ground-up clay give glints, a sense of alive earth, amenable but with energy. Is this why the stillness is so active? Tension between magnetic soil and a human attempt to hold such radiance?

"Two hundred years of leaves have wandered over him, incinerated by African light. He is far from his gleaming ground, but his royal gaze is timeless."—KCW

Galleries of clay commemorative sculpture were once assembled outside certain Akan villages. Images of heads and full figures were gathered in a forest necropolis called the "place of pots" *(asenie)*. The clay images were tended by royalty in memory of important men and women. As royal lineage members, it was their right to commission their own terracotta likenesses as they neared death.

Women were the primary, if not exclusive, ceramic artists sought for this task. They used a loamy clay body and mixed in a large portion of mica before beginning to hand-build the head in a hollow form. Through their work, the head evolved into a generalized portrait of the client with enough distinctive features to identify social status.

This head is that of a male elder and may have been attached to an entire body. Fine ridges ring his neck with folds of fat, illustrating a historic Akan aesthetic preference for such folds, a trait that identified the wealthy who ate well and led a privileged life. The elder's hair is depicted by twisted coils of clay in a hairstyle based on snail shells, perhaps an allegorical statement of this man's similarity to the peaceful, earthbound creature. Most of his head is shaved, a fashion adopted by male elders. The raised scarification on his cheeks may represent marks

designed to ward off malevolent forces. In keeping with Akan custom, his face is flawless, without any sign of age or imperfection. The client may have been reaching the end of his life, but his features are sealed at an eternal thirty.

When the client died, this image served in his funeral rites and was carried in a commemorative procession honoring the dead person. The funeral was held several weeks after a death and was a public occasion, attended by all who had known the deceased. Women sang mourning dirges to salute the accomplishments and character of the departed royal lineage members.

Eventually the clay image of this person was taken to the place of pots where it stood amidst other royal reminders of past importance. In the generation that followed, the *asenie* would be visited on a regular basis, and the image provided with food and drink. As time passed the clay heads were gradually abandoned and became submerged beneath layers of leaves and humus. Today, *asenie* sites with funerary terracottas have been located outside numerous Akan villages, some dating back to the seventeenth century. Archaeological excavations are beginning to establish a chronology and distribution for this major ceramic tradition.

37

15. Male and female figures
Ivory Coast
Kulango, 20th century
Wood, leather, beads, white chalk
deposits
H. 96.5 and 82.5 cm.
(38", 32 1/2")
81.17.225.1,.2

"In a tall unfolding, they act with serenity. The velvet of their smooth brown cellular forms is rimmed in white settling into the harsh crevices where touch cannot penetrate. Cicatrizations pull across the calves, the thighs, the heavy arched necks, the waiting faces. The scars stabilize, arresting the flow of surface, waking it up, catching light, stopping sight."—KCW

From an area of ethnic complexity, this pair of tall columnar figures shows signs of many stylizations. Their bodies are composed in an elongated formula of smooth brown segments carefully outlined in white. Hands are small and held tightly over their ribs to conform to the rising column. Facial features are confined to round eyes, a slender nose, and rectangular lips. All the joints are caked with white kaolin clay which may once have covered the entire surface. Clay was often mixed with herbs and water from rivers and applied to bodies and sculptures to signify a sacred state of purity and protection.

Although collected in 1967 in Wenchi, the territory of the Bron, this couple has been attributed to the work of the prolific Kulango. In a style that straddles many influences, the Kulango incorporate Lobi, Senufo, and Akan traits into a unique amalgamation. No account of the meaning or function of this couple is known. The prevalent use of figures in shrine houses honoring local deities may account for them. Despite being carved of hardwood, their feet have weathered away at the ankles, indicating that they stood upright for many years as was often the case for figures in shrine settings.

16. Mother and child figure
Zaire
Luba, 19th-20th century
Wood, metal
H. 50.2 cm. (19 3/4")
81.17.905

This icon of female fortitude addresses two converging roles. One is that of a respected first mother known in Luba myths of creation and legends of the founding of clans. Such a woman established the female line of succession and inheritance and became a dominant guardian of sacred emblems. To fulfill this important role, this woman is depicted with a calm dignity and down-to-earth solidity. The other role is that of an actual mother, whose agility must match the spry dexterity of the child who perches on her back. Children were carried this way when they were old enough to hold on, in days before cloth wraps were common. Sculpturally, the attitudes of a woman who is both resolute and vigorous are joined in this figure.

Luba female sculptures are known to have been used by individuals to ensure the birth of a first child and to protect a household from fire and witchcraft, and to ensure success in hunting and farming. The size and style of this example do not completely fit the usual Luba repertoire. Elements like the hatched coiffure, blue bead inset eyes, squared mouth and chin, and overall angular features are better known as Songe traits. They result in an unusual mixture with the rounded volumes and proportions of the Luba.

"How proud she is, striding the earth with the energy of a plow horse. How many children has she had? How many miles have those tough thighs carried her? What has that keen old face encountered with the tiny blue bead eyes that drill the air?

"Those high hard shoulders mean business—she carries her child as if it were a part of her anatomy, invisible like the end of her nose. She is part of the whole facade of women's faces. Her suffering, her laughter, her labor join together to become the impenetrable fabric of a village. She knows the role. She fits every nook and cranny with her ebullient mother-strength."

—KCW

41

17. Mother and child figure
(asie usu?)
Ivory Coast
Baule, late 19th-early 20th century
Wood
H. 66 cm. (26")
81.17.234

A svelte woman introduces an ideal Baule mother. Her body is a streamlined play of attenuated limbs that seem destined for hard work. Her strong neck is evidence of her developed ability to carry heavy loads on her head with ease. She holds her head high, the sign of one who is a productive and honorable member of her community. Finally, she carries the marks of a civilized personality in her carefully tended coiffure and scarification marks. Both are elements of decoration that require the cooperation of others to complete, and they thereby acknowledge her reliance on her community. Baule admiration for such a figure requires that an ideal beauty also be a person of high moral virtue.

The Baule artist strives for a moderate likeness, which is certainly evident in this mother. Her face is alert and well delineated, but not individualized. Her hair is depicted in fine rows of minute grooves and embellishments, but is not ornate. The scarification marks on her shoulders, back, and neck are precisely carved, but moderate in size and number. Each segment of her body is depicted, but not explicitly delineated.

Baule figures are made for particular purposes. This example is thought to have been carved for an

asie usu or nature spirit. Such spirits wander in the wilderness and reside in natural phenomena as untamed and unattractive entities. They may harbor malicious intentions and cause illness and disasters in farming and hunting. At times the spirit can form a bond with humans, causing them to tremble, fall into violent trances, and act as if possessed. In consultation with a diviner, the possessed individual may decide to commission a carved figure in order to lure the spirit into it. Some spirits dictate their preferences of wood to be used and form to be carved. Figures are often extremely beautiful in order to entice the spirit into appreciating it as a body worthy of habitation. Off and on, the "thing of the bush" will reside in the figure to receive its owner's attention and inducements for favors. If tamed with proper sacrifice, the figure may bring the owner success and reduce his chances of failure in many endeavors.

The asie usu was kept by an individual in his or her room as a private shrine. It would have been offered food and libations throughout the owner's lifetime. Through the carved figure, the Baule had a measure of control over the antisocial, unpredictable elements of life.

18. Mother and child figure
Oshogbo, Nigeria
Yoruba, 19th century
Wood, glass beads
H. 43.2 cm. (17″)
81.17.594

"Perfection at standstill. All surfaces are solemn, effaced to a supple sequence of angles, active curves and spaces as exquisitely modeled as the substance. Wood has been changed into a concentrate, a spiritual essence which no intellect can touch. The woman is almost too sweet to know by fingertips, each slippery softness glides away, vanishing into the next set of swift and delicate surfaces."—KCW

44

Countless hands have praised this masterful mother and child. Her face has been caressed again and again, dissolving her features into subtle suggestions of a demure countenance. Her body has been rubbed, leaving behind a warm softening of each surface. Fingers virtually melt into place at her shoulders and around the bowl. Meanwhile, the original artwork continues to unfold. Her baby peeks out, vertically balancing his mother's crouched posture. She is captured as a gesture of calm capability, fulfilling several roles at once.

Her main duty is to serve Shango, to whom she is visibly devoted. Two thunderbolts issue from her head to signify his presence. Shango, the thunder god, is as wild and tempestuous as she is benign and thoughtful. A segment of a praise poem to him reveals a sense of his character:

The god who imparts his beauty
to the women with whom he sleeps,
He takes his neighbor's roof
and covers his own head.
He lends money and does not ask it
  back.
If you do not offer him a seat
he will sit on top of your nose.
If you do not share your maize gruel
  with him
he will slip under your finger nail
and take his share.
Shango does as he pleases.

(Beier, 1970, p. 32)

It is clear that Shango has a tendency toward the tyrannical. Most of the time he waits in the heavens with thunder and lightning bolts at hand, ready to strike down anyone he chooses, but usually criminals. Despite his brutality Shango may be persuaded to occasional benevolence. When his altar is tended and his shrine is occupied by female devotees, Shango may favor humanity and not only spare them from his wrath, but be generous with his protection. This sculpture would have stood amidst an accumulated ensemble of ritual implements and sculptures for Shango. Priests and priestesses devoted to Shango performed sacrifices and voiced praise and invocations to him.

Sculptural female followers may try to entice Shango into refraining from violence. The motif of the child on the mother's back may suggest to Shango that he should protect his devotees like a mother who protects her child. This woman entreats him with a parable of excellence in appearance and character. She has absorbed the splitting potency of the lightning bolts at the top of her head, but she continues to support her child and to hold out a bowl of offerings. She has learned how to take the capricious power of Shango and wield it to intensify her life.

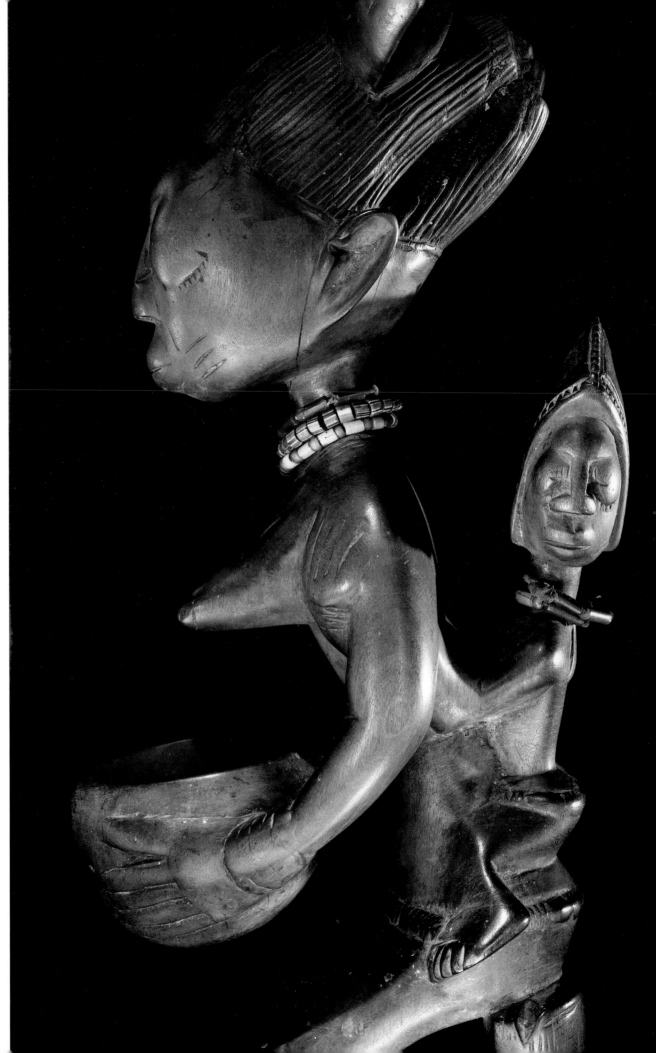

Lines and volumes converge on this woman's distended abdomen to assert that it is the center of her concern. Shoulder blades have merged with breasts, hands point forward, and the pegged patterning targets her umbilicus. Beyond her central focus, she also wears the signs of a Kaka woman. Her hair is arranged in a crest of rounded hair, she has guinea-corn stalks to simulate ear and nose plugs, and her body is adorned with rows of iron pegs representing a sequence of raised welts. Kaka blacksmiths contributed the many pegs to emulate the cicatrization pattern common to the region.

Women offered libations of palm wine to this figure to enhance their fecundity. The wine was poured into a hole at the top of the figure's head. Palm wine is a highly nutritious liquid which the Kaka drink with daily meals, and enjoy as an intoxicating beverage when it is fermented. The usual Kaka family routine included the pouring of libations each morning and evening to honor the ancestors that are attended by the immediate family. Extended families also had shrines tended by priests; a short pole inserted into the hollow core of this figure would have established its position in a shrine. Whether it served one family or a larger group is not known.

20. Female figure
Nigeria
Igbo, 20th century
Wood, pigment, mirrored glass
H. 122 cm. (48″)
81.17.525

"She is a tall presence, closed in ceremony. Every signal is tightly fit in place. Legs are immobilized in enormous jewelry, hands are heavy with precise symbolic objects. The stance is measured in millimeters of gesture, the face is white and cold, chilled by a command for silence."—KCW

This accomplished Igbo maiden is decorated and dressed in layers of costume. Her entire appearance attests to hours spent on cosmetic artistry. Her hair, stiffened with a traditional pomade, is molded into an intricate composition of plaited fringe, central crest, and mirrors which have been sewn into the sides. Her face is painted white as a sign of her sacred poise. The final stage in her makeup covers not only her face but her entire body. Using a stain derived from indigo *(uli)*, a woman and her assistants executed the minute lines of body painting. Ivory and brass armlets, anklets, and waist bands imply that she is wealthy.

The raised scars accenting her stout stomach firmly identify her. Rows of rectangular marks, such as are commonly cut into the skin of a young woman before her marriage, lead down her torso. Her rotund figure results from months of intentional overeating in the seclusion of a special "fattening house" *(nkpu)*, a period intended to prepare a woman for life as a mature wife.

Many similarly embellished brides-to-be paraded and danced about the village in a vainglorious time of appreciation. One source

mentions that the women carried the tufted end of a cow's tail mounted on leather and a hand-held mirror at this time (Basden, 1921, p. 224). Holding a mirror that best suits the Western notion of cosmetics—from the neck up—they appeared emblazoned from head to foot in a cosmetic cavalcade. They maintained an erect carriage and calm expression, possibly connoting a character of inner quiet. Igbo women who combined such outer and inner beauty were lauded in sculpture and praise-salutes:

Young lady, you are:
A mirror that must not go out in the sun
A child that must not be touched by dew
One that is dressed up in hair
A lamp with which people find their way
Moon that shines bright
An eagle feather worn by a husband
A straight line drawn by God.
(Egudu and Mwoga, 1973, p. 20)

This sculptural image of an Igbo maiden may have served as the centerpiece for a voluntary dance association.

21. Female figure
Nigeria
Igbo?/Ibibio, 20th century
Wood, pigment
H. 49.8 cm. (19 1/2″)
81.17.516

Muted remnants of black calligraphy cover this woman's body. She thereby symbolically documents a period in an Igbo woman's life when ample decoration was extremely important. Before marriage a girl entered what has been called a "fattening house." Contrary to early twentieth century records which underrate this practice as one designed to produce "swollen specimens of femininity" for parade, the fattening house had considerable educational value. In its seclusion older women taught the younger girls many arts and duties—singing, dancing, cosmetics, cooking. The art of painting elaborate patterns in black pigment made from natural sources was a collaborative effort among women. These dyes were temporary; a design might remain visible from two weeks to a few months. At their debut, the young women displayed to their audience the temperament and stylish appearance they had learned was appropriate to their sex.

This figure is aligned in a tight, crouched pose. Her body has been re-invented in a series of geometric parts—cones and cylinders and a curving crest of hair—which documents a form of hairdressing using clay, charcoal, and oil. This figure resembles carvings worn by men as headdresses in Ogbom ceremonies to honor the earth deity Ala. Every other year, Ogbom was performed before the shrine of Ala or a central clearing as a joyous recognition of her part in helping to make children plentiful. Before the performance, the carvings were decorated with body painting (uri) designs. Without the signs of having been outfitted as a headdress, however, this figure may also have been used by a diviner or herbalist in a shrine.

"She's dancing!

"She comes out of the earth performing akimbo a shuffle step as if some warm magnetic wave poured through her soles. Yet, how straight she is. Her back is tough and sure, welded to tight arms and legs. Her big rubbery smile is fixed but gentle and her mirror eyes follow the distance."

—KCW

It is obvious that this figure does not duplicate the actual appearance of a Toma woman. Instead it presents the features of a personalized spirit. The distinctive face, with its flat cheek planes and slit mouth, strongly resembles a Toma mask known as Landai, a terrifying spirit involved with men's initiation who was not ever to be seen by women. Beneath the face, the figure bears traces of scarification marks on her stomach and an apron indicative of her status as an initiated woman. This amalgamation of a spirit's face and a female body may result from the conventions of Toma carving or derive from the request of a specific spirit being.

Figurative images were often supplied for a spirit who came to an individual and wished to begin a relationship. The spirit frequently suggested the character of the carving it desired. In return for providing this personalized form, the human benefactor expected to obtain special abilities and protection from illness and disasters from the spirit, who would then take up residence in the image.

22. Female figure
Guinea/Liberia
Toma/Loma, 20th century
Wood, metal, beads, fiber
H. 63.5 cm. (25″)
81.17.182

53

23. Power figure *(nkisi)*
Zaire
Kongo, 19th-20th century
Wood, pigment, mirror, glass
H. 24.5 cm. (9 5/8″)
81.17.835

A sculptor and a diviner/healer/priest *(nganga)* collaborated to create this image of a vain White officer. He wears a tuxedo, delineated explicitly in the back, holds a flintlock rifle, and sits upon a bench. When taken to the *nganga*, the sculpture was consecrated with effective ingredients, designed to capture a soul within. The *nganga*'s additional medicines *(bilongo)* have caused this officer's shoulders to swell into enormous epaulets. Reeds which may contain gunpowder are plastered onto the stomach with a resinous mass to become a gland of power. A mirror has been embedded into the gland to cause the reflection of evil and to facilitate a diviner telling future events by looking into the *nkisi*.

Nkisi were put to use as a calculated form of therapy, often to address so-called anger illnesses. The *nganga* specified treatment to cure not only the physical manifestations of pain, but the anger associated with the pain. Clients working with *nkisi* had a means of metaphoric and metonymic therapy at hand. Formulas of speech and activation of the *nkisi*'s force ensured that their anger could be turned against the wrath or witchcraft contributing to their pain. Individuals also kept *nkisi* for general benevolent purposes—to aid them in hunting, trade, ensuring fidelity, and having many offspring.

54

"Many times collected by non-Africans, the labels on this piece keep attempting his identity. He ... has a finger in many pies. His gun, his hat, his pallor, his britches, the lovely tails of his coat ... bespeak of White. He is alone with his petulant mouth and his pigeon toes. Given a White man's face, the thick mirrored poultices pull his arrogant weight away to make a precious morsel of imagination available."

—KCW

55

24. Divination container
(opon igede Ifa)
Master Areogun (c. 1880-1956)
Osi-Ilorin, Nigeria
Ekiti Yoruba, 20th century
Wood
H. 55.9 cm. (22″)
81.17.621a,b

When problems arise or decisions must be made, the Yoruba often turn to a priest of divination *(babalawo)* for assistance. In private consultation, the *babalawo* calls upon the oracle of fate, *Ifa* and its 256 marked verses *(odu),* to derive a corpus of religious and philosophical thought from which to draw. Implements for the divination ritual are kept in a large covered bowl like this one. The *babalawo* takes palm nuts from the bowl and manipulates them to indicate which section of the vast *Ifa* oracle should be recited. The *babalawo* narrates the appropriate verse, and through it the cli-ent is given a glimpse of the future and how best to alleviate the current problem.

Solutions usually take the form of sacrifices and prescribed ritual actions. One short *odu* describes the need for sacrifice:

Osu, the brightly shining one, Ifa
     priest of the Earth,
Performed Ifa divination for the
     Earth.
The Earth was told to stop perform-
     ing sacrifices intended to make
     him wealthy,
But to perform instead the sacrifice
     which would protect him against
     his enemies.

We are certainly alive,
And we are pleading
That as long as we remain on the
   Earth,
The Earth may never be destroyed.
                    (Abimbola, 1977, p. 111)

Many ritual objects are carved for
the *babalawo's* use. This container
has five interior compartments for
the storage of palm nuts, divining
chains, kola nuts, cowrie shells, and
other small accessories. Its exterior
has been transformed into a contin-
uous relief by a master carver,
Areogun, who is known to have
carved two similar bowls. A thick

impasto crust muddies and softens
all the linear details of the relief sur-
face. Deciphering the sequence of
figures requires looking at the over-
all outlines and disregarding pro-
portions, which are stretched to
encompass the bowl's surfaces.
Rifles and pistols tend to be enor-
mously overscaled.

Two figures dominate the upper
register: a man on horseback and a
man on a bicycle. Smoking a pipe
and transporting a package tied to
the back of the bike, the cyclist
probably represents Eshu, the mis-
chievous messenger to the gods. The
movements of these two figures are

held in check by two soldiers bat-
tling over a woman, a woman offer-
ing a calabash, and a soldier holding
the reins of the horseman. The bot-
tom register depicts a mixture of
peaceful and troublesome indi-
viduals: a *dun-dun* drummer,
woman, fan-holder, and pipe-smoker
are interspersed between a warrior
raising a cudgel to begin a fight, a
soldier with a rifle, and a warrior
leader (Ologun) with raised sword
and spear. People on the move or in
an agitated profile posture are
counteracted by those who stand
still, looking directly at the viewer.

No narrative is implied by the

sequence. However, in keeping with
the concerns of *Ifa*, there are allu-
sions to some of the problems
addressed during divination. Con-
flicts needing resolution, journeys of
uncertain outcome, those who give
and those who demand, creative and
destructive personalities may all
have been discussed in consultation
with the *babalawo*. If such changes
and needs become a strain on an
individual's composure, they can
call on the wisdom of *Ifa* to give
them divine assistance in clarifying
their problems and suggesting
solutions.

25. Staff (Eshu)
Bamgboye of Odo-Owa
Nigeria
Ekiti Yoruba, 20th century
Wood, twine
H. 42.9 cm. (16 7/8")
81.17.598

This figure abounds with ambiguity, as is befitting a representative of Eshu who is known to be belligerent and solemn, ribald and revealing, a maker of mischief and miracles. In simple terms, he is the trickster of the Yoruba pantheon of deities. No one can predict his next move or his next shift in meaning.

An investigation of this sculpture reveals many of Eshu's attributes. Taking a flute to his lips, Eshu may play a soft, alluring tune or a wild accompaniment to his own erratic dance. With his flute he can act as the divine messenger who clears the way to the other gods, or Eshu can choose to use it as an instrument of defiance, blowing it in one of his many acts of irreverence toward authority.

If so inclined, Eshu might also grasp the calabashes (oogun) attached to the crown of his arching hairstyle. In each long-necked calabash he keeps numerous medicines and charms to enable him to put people to sleep, to become invisible, or to transform himself into another creature. One story about Eshu's exploits exemplifies his magical propensities:

Orunmila had fallen in love with Earth and was told that a sacrifice including a rat would enable him to marry her. Doing as he was told, Orunmila added some common beads to a rat corpse in the forest. Earth, meanwhile, wore 200 cloths about her waist and declared that

she would only marry someone who saw her bare buttocks. On the day after Orunmila's sacrifice, Earth went into the forest. Suddenly Eshu clapped his hands, causing the rat to come alive and turning the beads tied to the rat into precious ones. Earth began to chase the rat with its valuable jewelry and did not notice that all 200 cloths were falling from her waist, until she was naked. When Orunmila came by to inspect his sacrifice, he met Earth running around naked. Earth soon became Orunmila's wife (Bascom, 1969, pp. 155-57). In this act of deception Eshu created momentary chaos which carried a blessing in disguise.

Eshu carefully tends his long arching hair, which indicates his libidinous and unrestrained powers. It has grown to an enormously exaggerated size and complexity with a crisscrossing pattern of braids. At the tip of the coiffure Eshu executes his final act of contradiction. A bearded face, presumably that of an elder, becomes a Janus counterpart. Two sides to Eshu's personality are commemorated, the erratic and the wise.

Many Yoruba make a habit of incorporating Eshu's presence into their lives. Sacrifices to him at crossroads and markets, and priests who carry staffs like this one, are commonplace. Despite his popularity Eshu defies exact description. Getting to know him is a test of one's tolerance for ambiguity.

"Quickly the face gathers attention. ... The eyes in particular have a mixture of belligerence and solitude. They are the first things that come alive when a human hand wakes the wood. The black jelly sees. He is up to something.

"... The giant headdress is busy, wires squeal the codes which only the initiated know. Eshu is an IBM, a primordial hot line. Watch him with affection, if not a little awe." —KCW

26. Feast-making spoon
(wunkirmian)
Liberia/Ivory Coast
Dan, 20th century
Wood, iron
H. 61.6 cm. (24 1/4")
81.17.204

An extremely generous Dan woman once owned this spoon. She carried it as an emblem of her virtue as the most hospitable woman of her clan *(wunkirle)*. To earn this distinction, she had to be recognized as an extremely efficient and amiable woman. Whenever necessary, a *wunkirle* would provide ample food and housing for guests in the village. Her fame and success grew as her spirit of giving grew. Men recognized her talent when she provided for travelling dance troupes, merit festivals, and for those who worked at clearing the fields. Women of the village esteemed her intelligence and accomplishments as well.

Most of the year the spoon hung on the wall in the *wunkirle*'s home. The incised chameleon/lizard depicted on its back is a creature of the soil and an intermediary to aid in the quest for fertility. It forms the reverse side of a large scoop called the "pregnant with rice belly" (Fischer and Himmelheber, 1976, p. 157). The legs, with a buoyant muscular stance, tell of the physical strength and willingness the *wunkirle* needs to support her role.

Festivals in honor of the *wunkirle* allow the women to carry the spoons as staffs of distinction. In honor of their extraordinary status, they arrive dancing and singing attired in men's clothing because, in their words, "only men are taken seriously" (Fischer and Himmelheber, 1976, p. 159). Attendants escort them and sing, and throw rice, peanuts, and coins to the audience. As other *wunkirle* assemble, the festival becomes a dramatic competition of extravagant giving. By the day's end, the woman of the highest order of generosity is proclaimed, with the spoon as her scepter. As a final tribute, men wearing masks sing to honor her gracious reputation.

27. Janus-faced figure
(Sakimatwematwe)
Zaire
Lega, 19th-20th century
Wood, pigment
H. 28.3 cm. (11 1/8″)
81.17.862

"The gentlest edges of African carving come into focus with the caress of hands. The older they are the deeper the brilliance, the more smothered in kaolin and use, the higher the intuitive force becomes.

"Faces are fit together like tight winter leaf forms. Their slow rectangles open, the eyes see, the nose divides, the small mouth barely utters. Severe as Gothic nuns they peer from their tight captivity. Like prisms their faces search. For once the four corners of the world meet."—KCW

An instructor of a high grade of Lega culture once drew this figure from a basket, rubbed it with white kaolin clay, and displayed it to initiates. He may have interpreted it through dance or song, or placed it on a mat to contemplate its meaning. Four sets of Lega eyes then scanned their audience to discern who had the values they must affirm.

One aphorism associated with this type of Janus-headed figure is that of Sakimatwematwe or "Mr. Many-Heads who has seen an elephant on the far side of the large river." The discerning vision of one who sees in many directions with wisdom and knowledge is thereby commended. This penetrating omniscience may also imply that one should not talk behind the back of Lega aristocrats, for they are not easily fooled.

Such condensed lessons, combining artwork with proverbial teaching, are a pervasive aspect of Lega life. Individuals who seek to hold office and authority are required to incorporate such teachings into their own lives. Only candidates who demonstrate a moral aptitude are allowed to proceed to higher grades of power. As one ascended through the grades of Lega learning, artwork like this might be required as an insignia of rank.

28. Belt mask in leopard form
Nigeria
Benin, 16th century
Ivory, brass
H. 17.8 cm. (7")
81.17.494

"There's a malicious grin in this one.... His lips quiver, his eyes are merry, his ears are like delicate leaves. The ivory is deep, smoothed ... to a hand-smothered caramel.... Studs ... become his royal trappings, adding savagery, armor, power, even terror to the sleek innocence of his luminosity."—KCW

In the sixteenth and seventeenth centuries, a monarch (Oba) of Benin was surrounded by an array of leopard imagery. Pairs of life-size ivory and brass leopards sat beside him at court functions. Live leopards were kept in captivity and tamed by a special guild that paraded them in chains before the Oba during an annual procession. Leopard pelts were under the Oba's exclusive control and worn only with his permission. Leopard faces cast as maskettes and leopard teeth assembled into necklaces were emblems of his authority. Any leopard caught or killed was presented to the Oba immediately. The metaphorical link between the "King of the Bush" and the "King of the Home" was established over several centuries. A praise song for the Oba of Benin recorded in 1961 is indicative of this long-standing alliance:

King of the world
Leopard, king of the world
King of the world who seizes one
   swiftly
Leopard who catches its prey in
   broad daylight.
          (Ben-Amos, 1983, p. 51)

Just as the leopard can stalk his prey and attack with swift force, so the Oba can wield decisive aggression when necessary. Their leadership capabilities are considered similar in Bini references. Leopards, like Obas, keep a royal disposition, exercising restraint before they choose to make a striking advance. Their royal countenance was also thought to derive from their good nature and ability to call other animals into orderly meetings and discussions. As leaders, the leopard and Oba were approached with a similar mixture of affection and terror.

Leopard faces were used as awe-inspiring insignia. This ivory example was probably worn around the waist of an Oba of the sixteenth century. Thin brass inlays convincingly capture the glint of feline eyes, and brass studs simulate a spotted coat. Layers of accumulated reddish oil have saturated the ivory and created its rich, gleaming surface. Recently, in a ritual which derives from older Benin tradition, the Oba has worn similar ivory masks. A festival called Emobo is a relatively solemn "spirit-dismissing ceremony" which takes place in the midst of an annual cycle of appearances by the Oba. For Emobo, "the oba sits in a specially constructed pavilion made of red cloth—red being a threatening color, one with the capacity to drive away evil. Later he dances with an ivory gong, striking it to repel malevolent spirits" (Ben-Amos, 1980, pp. 89, 93). Ivory leopard faces seem to be a protective part of the Oba's regalia during Emobo, proclaiming visibly the Oba/leopard link as they have for centuries.

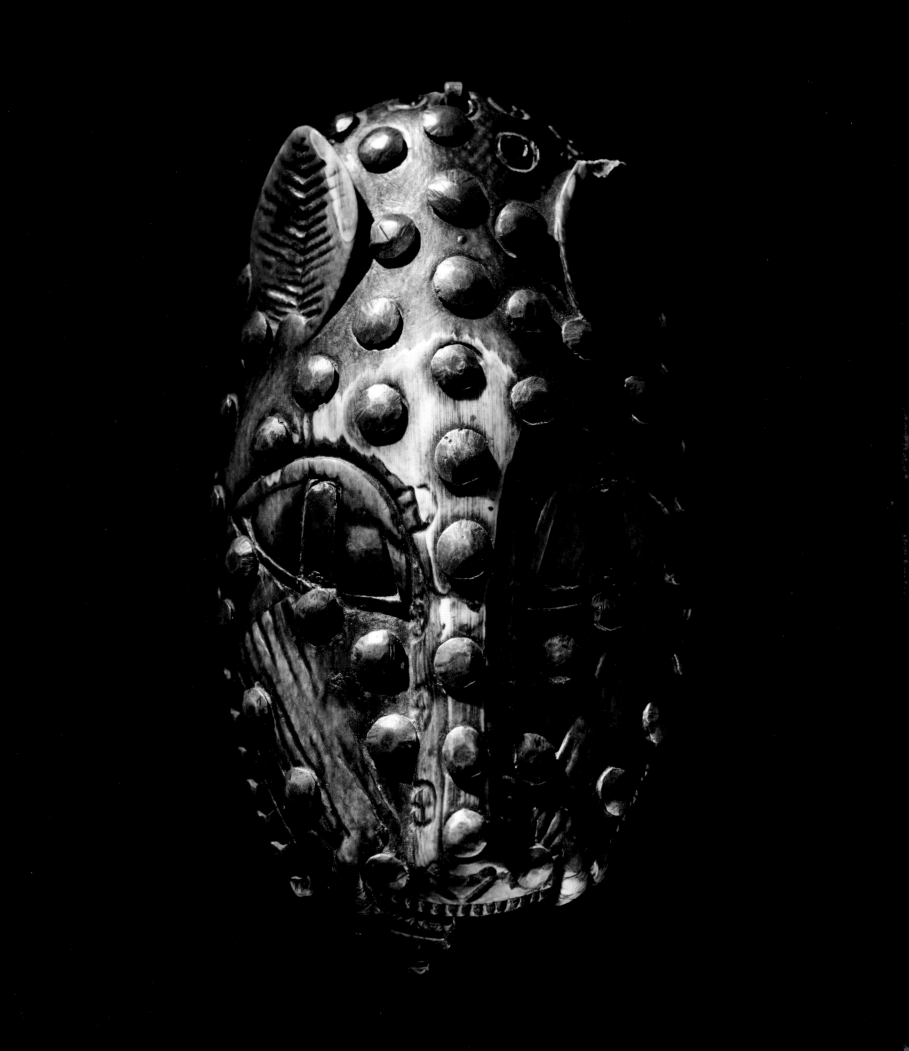

One man stands at the pinnacle of authority in the Kom kingdom, the Fon. One artwork is critical in validating his role, the throne. Here, a Kom queen is given life-size tribute and united to a cylindrical stool. Her image becomes a sculptural representation of a lineage of queen mothers *(nafon)* who presided beside their sons during their reigns as Fons. She provides a visible link with a long complex chain of Kom history.

This throne was carved sometime in the last century, either during the reign of Fon Yuh (1865-1912) or his great-grandfather, Fon Nkwain (c. 1825). It was collected in Laikom, the Kom capital, where it was housed within the premises of Fon Yuh. The throne was part of a triad of the Fon's ancestors memorialized in sculptural stool form, the others representing his father and his first wife. The queen throne reinforced the Fon's alliance with two females who contributed to the legitimacy of his bloodline. Bo, the female founder of the Kom dynasty who led the people through a series of disasters traced back to the 1800s, is present in idealized form. Her identity is augmented by that of the actual mother of the Fon, who served in real life as one of his chief advisors.

A German expedition acquired this throne and its male counterpart in 1904 and gave them to the Museum für Völkerkunde, Frankfurt. They remained together until 1934, when the female began an odyssey of ownership through the Speyer Collection, Berlin, the Rat-ton Collection, Paris, and finally came to the White Collection in 1966. This throne and its Frankfurt mate are the oldest surviving Kom throne figures known to exist.

The queen's image, presently spare and roughly hewn, is likely to have been far more conspicious at an earlier time. Cylindrical cut glass beads sewn in solid profusion would have once covered her body, but now only a residual collar of blue-and-white checkerboard pattern seed beads and tack holes attest to her former ornamentation. A copper sheet overlay covers her face, ears, and hands, as they would not have been covered by the beading. Her eyes are formed of a resinous substance and outlined with tin strips. Camwood powder residue coats her ears. In a gesture of salutation, she clasps her right hand over her left, a gesture that also implies the presentation of kola nuts to the Fon.

Primarily kept in the Fon's private chambers, the thrones emerged periodically on public view as a symbol of the continuity of royal succession. During annual ceremonies to pay tribute to royal ancestors, the thrones played a major role in validation of the proceedings. Their presence may have been similarly useful at palavers and meetings of the councils of royal clan members and commoner lords who met with the Fon. Their use as private furnishings may also have been extensive.

(The throne will not be included in the national tour of the exhibition.)

29. Throne of a queen
Laikom, Bamenda Division,
Cameroon
Kom, 19th century
Wood, beads, string, leather, hair,
metal, hide, pigment
H. 173.4 cm. (68 1/4")
81.17.718

67

30. Retainer figure
Cameroon
Kom, 19th century
Wood, cloth fragments, nail
H. 76.2 cm. (30″)
81.17.719

68

"How gracefully he comes together. Every stroke of the adze signals mastery. Tensions arrive at points of inertia. Watch the arm move to the huge looming hand and its calm floating bowl. Watch the legs bend in a lithe curve to the feet, forming a doorway in which to catch the leopard. Even the back pours upward, suspending the luminous face and the laughing eyes. Everywhere the adze improvises, touching the intellect with a light, guiding skill, twisting asymmetry to happiness."

—KCW

This figure offered bowls full of delicacies to those permitted to enter the inner sanctum of Kom royalty. Palm wine was dispensed from one bowl, while the smaller gourd-shaped bowl provided kola nuts. When the king (Fon) of Kom began a formal meeting, he might designate that the retainer appear. It also would be brought out from a secured treasury room for state occasions, when it also served as a receptacle for camwood to anoint the Fon. During events of public display, it joined many other royal art forms in an opulent panoply drawn from the Fon's treasury.

At one time, a beaded cloth was tightly sewn over the wooden figure from the neck down. Small tacks and remnants of burlap are one indication of the lost beading. More noticeably, the minutely faceted surface of the adzed carving is rough, an indication that it was intended to be covered. Despite the lack of beading, the figure's distinguished bearing is evident in his attributes and attitude. He wears the knobbed cap of a Kom nobleman and he sits on a leopard stool. Leopards are a prerogative of royalty; their emblematic use was restricted for persons of exalted rank. Rank is also displayed by his seated posture. Permission to sit in the Fon's presence was rarely granted. In a calm display of authority, this man exemplifies an

esteemed associate of Kom royalty.

The rigid social structure of the Kom kingdom made exceptions for one offical not born to royal status. Retainers *(chinda)* in personal service to the Fon were a normal part of the palace staff. Initially they came as commoner children to do mundane tasks, but might eventually become highly respected advisors to the Fon after years of devoted service.

Tentatively dated to the nineteenth century, this retainer figure was last photographed in the field in 1953-1960 amid a number of royal Kom throne figures in a storage chamber in Laikom.

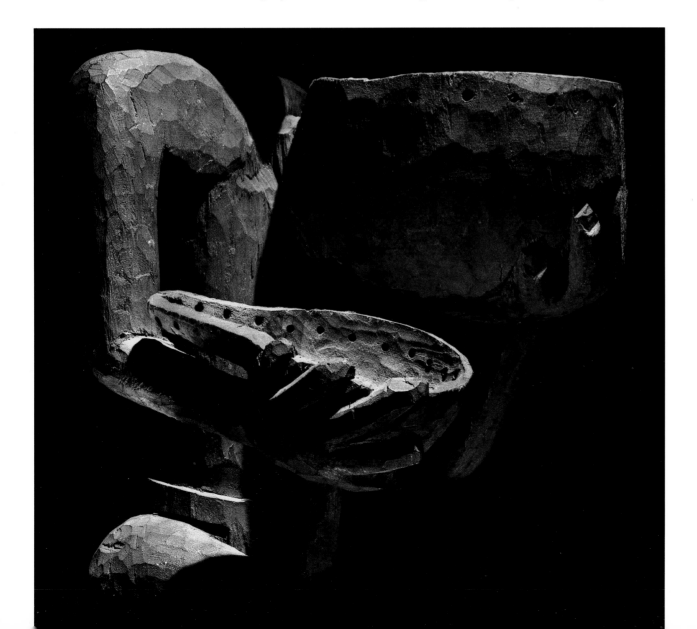

"They are a pair of turreted skyscrapers.... Horns twirl like staircases above a whole architecture, springing buttresses and sudden pendentives.... Poised on an attenuated neck is the mother's face, with studded eyes squeezed on either side in prim consternation.

"Her fawn, perched like a fond repeat, has the same sequence of planes and angles. Spontaneously young, he still assumes the silhouette of the archetype. He switches his ears upward and snorts with joy. The tilt of his legs lets him prance and bounce. His blackness is dented with a soft dapple, joining his round torpedo tail with the flair of his baby mane."—KCW

African art is epitomized for many Westerners by the abstract antelope headress called Tjiwara or Chi Wara. French administrators first collected them in the 1930s and encouraged their production for export.

Bamana beliefs enlarge the scope of the Tjiwara aesthetic to include many practical, social, and philosophical teachings. One thorough analysis of Tjiwara describes a vast "symbolic scaffolding" which supports this tradition (Zahan, 1980). It begins with the selection of wood to be carved, usually of the *nguna* tree, a tree thought to have furnished the Bamana with fruit before the invention of agriculture. Next the manner of carving is considered. Bamana tenets prescribe that the headdress show precision and clarity *(jayan)*. Just as the Bamana value straightforward discernability in people, so they strive to maintain those values in certain art forms. Accordingly, the Tjiwara is conceived in a series of angular abbreviations which condense the essential character of an antelope and reduce it to a clear abstract equivalent.

A specific antelope, the female oryx, is depicted due to many biological and behavioral associations. Tapering spiral horns shoot straight up to remind the eastern Bamana of the sprouting grains— *fonio*, millet, and sorrel—that are the major food crops of their area. The female of this species is also known to have a nine-month gestation period for a single offspring. She is also considered a model of fidelity and obedience in relations with her mate. In performances, the female masker always appears with her spouse; they dance as an inseparable pair to indicate the marital cooperation necessary for successful farming. The female oryx is also said to be associated with the earth as a positive provider—fertile, nurturing, generous in spirit, and willing to carry her "sons" on her back as this headdress shows. Another unusual trait of the oryx is that it is astonishingly resistant to thirst and can go without water for long periods. By analogy, it is hoped that the earth will withstand droughts and still support Bamana farming.

Tjiwara performers wear a fiber mane said to symbolize rain, and carry a pair of sticks to symbolize the rays of the sun. The performers enter a field leaning on the sticks and dig diligently for hours while crowds gather. Through songs, the audience encourages the Tjiwara's devotion to the labor necessary to cultivate the dry savannah of the Bamana homeland.

Men and women openly contribute to the Tjiwara masquerade each year, and still continue to do so. Artistically, Tjiwara advocates agricultural practices that are meant to ensure a bountiful harvest. The importance of a good crop is conveyed in one myth in which a water spirit appears before the future king of the Segou kingdom, leads him to his watery domain, and shows him a piece of gold, a piece of silver, other precious substances, and then a pile of grain saying: "Choose. Gold and silver are wealth ... grain is power" (Zahan, 1980, p. 135).

31. Female antelope headdress
(Tjiwara *muso)*
Mali
Bamana, 19th century
Wood, metal, fiber
H. 87.6 cm. (34 1/2″)
81.17.23

32. Mask *(bolo)*
Upper Volta
Bobo, 20th century
Wood, hair, pigment
H. 47 cm. (18 1/2")
81.17.87

"He is a gladiator armored with keloids of cracks, scars, and paint that weathered long ago.... Like the process of petrification, age replaces sap with stains of earth, and the oily salt of ceremonial sweat.... One eye gazes in a hard square squint. The other hides in the ... sudden wistfulness of an eyelash, long horsehair gummed to the lid and trimmed....

"He was killed. That hole smashed his head to make him a shell, an old dead piece of carved tree no longer recognizable as a usable thing.... A newer mask performs. A newer set of leaves sway, new raffia skirts swish. Let them. This old fellow stays."—KCW

After a harvest season, Bobo farmers welcome a season of masks which arrives in numerous versions of leaf, fiber, and wood types. They are all believed to be visual manifestations of Dwo, the son of God, who was sent to restore order when chaos threatened after God withdrew from earth. All the masks also represent forces of the bush—the spontaneous, undisciplined growth that human society opposes with its ordered nature, yet is dependent on for food.

In the Bobo hierarchy, masks made of tied leaves take precedence over masks of wood. Leaf masks *(soxo)* appear first in a sequence and are felt to be the most potent concentration of vegetative force. Their performance is always required to assure recognition of the immense power that Wuro has conceded to men, allowing them to farm and to make use of the vital impulses of the vegetal realms. Such masks are buried in the bush on the same evening of the ceremony in which they officiate. Fiber masks are next, followed by the anthropomorphic wooden masks.

Unlike the *soxo* masks, the wood masks worn with fiber manes seem to act primarily as entertainment. This particular mask, the *bolo*, has been adapted by the Bobo from their Zara neighbors. It is a type also present at funeral ceremonies *(sakon)*, but their precise role is not well known.

"Physical ebullience pours through her. Her huge round softnesses are strictly kept by carefully crisp surfaces, sudden stops and turns. Her shoulders dominate at a glance. At another, from the side, it is a shelf of buttocks, the heavy bosom held in check by a towering round head with a crest of curving hair."—KCW

Masks topped by images of young women dance to honor deceased Mossi female elders. The term *karan* connotes the mask type and perhaps the "ancestor-who-hides-herself-behind-something." *Wemba* designates an elderly widow who has left her husband's clan after his death to return and live with her own clan. As a *wemba*, she assumes a position of respect as she is closely approaching the realm of ancestral spirits.

When she dies, the mask dances in her funeral, to encourage her soul *(sigha)* to leave the compound and join other ancestors. The *karan-wemba* escorts the corpse to verify that proper burial is taking place, and then reappears at a later formal funeral celebration in the dry season. When not appearing before public audiences, the masks were stored in the clan house and might receive sacrifices to the *wemba* whose memory they serve.

Two examples of *karan-wemba* illustrate its regional range (cat. nos. 33, 34). This mask with a concave face and a fuller proportioned figure is attributed to the Yatenga area of Upper Volta. The hair of the figure is coiffed in a sagittal crest *(gyonfo)*, once in vogue among Mossi women. On her back, a sequence of incised sections suggest scarification patterns, or raised keloids executed in rows. Her bountiful youth becomes a masked compliment to the female elders who raised her.

33. Mask with female figure
(karan-wemba)
Yatenga region, Upper Volta
Mossi, 20th century
Wood
H. 99 cm. (39")
81.17.109

75

This second Mossi mask, from the Risiam area, has a convex face supporting a sinewy figure with a plank extension. Its blending of the double-zigzag pierced plank with a straight-shouldered, animated female support is elegantly attenuated. One Mossi comment has been offered to explain the openwork design of the plank: that it signifies "the way of the road of the dance with the dead" (Schweeger-Hefel, 1980, p. 326). This remark may allude to the belief that masks provide a way of communicating with ancestors.

Risiam-area masks have been observed at both male and female funerals. Their costume consists of a mantle of cloth or a black fiber fringe. A short stick inserted in the mouth region would be held by the dancer in his teeth as he balanced the towering height of the mask. One description of the funeral of an earth priest *(tenga soba)* enables us to visualize the mask in performance:

Each of the masks danced in turn, accompanied by the clan drummers, in a small oval dance area defined by the large tightly packed crowd which had assembled.... The mask moved back and forth between the group of elders and drummers at one end of the dance area.... As each mask approached the extremity of the dance area, the mask wearer suddenly stopped and rotated his neck so that the upper part of the plank swept a large arc. The motion was at the same time graceful and violent.

(Roy, 1979, p. 191)

34. Mask with female figure (karan-wemba)
Upper Volta
Mossi, 20th century
Wood, pigment
H. 137.8 cm. (54 1/4")
81.17.112

35. Gelede mask
Amosa Akapo of Igbe Quarter,
Igbesa
Nigeria
Awori Yoruba, 20th century
Wood, pigment
H. 20.2 cm. (8″)
81.17.585

"Lacquer and Islam coat this face as if to cool it. The thin lacquer surface is European. Fastidious collectors of earlier decades reacted well to shining things: table tops, floors, and art should be immaculate. So Africa was polished to please.

"Islam is a deeper presence. Arabs and Africans met for centuries to exchange not only ivory, salt, slaves, and gold, but ways of life. Diverse as they are, antagonisms understood are kept alive. Alufa, the Hausa priest, would evolve as an African, but with edges honed by the sharp thin light of Arab steel."—KCW

Each spring, Yoruba men present an extensive masquerade to honor and placate women. They are compelled to do so by a tradition of concern for *aje* or the mystical powers of womanhood. The Yoruba perceive that many women have inscrutable facades which hide reservoirs of intense spiritual strength. These women may interact daily with the community around them, but react secretly to the pompous, impolite, and cruel actions of men in their midst. If so angered by men's selfish ways, these women may turn their reserves of strength against men and destroy them. Crops may fail, sickness may overcome children, an epidemic may strike, all due to a woman's *aje*. In this way, the powers of alienated women threaten to destroy the joy of Yoruba life.

To counteract this potential disaster, men call upon Gelede to remedy ill will. The presence of negative *aje* is said to melt as the women are pampered by the attention and energy directed toward them during the Gelede performance. Elderly women are pleased as the dancers always seek their approval, acknowledge their importance, and address the imbalances which exist in Yoruba society. Gelede encourages men to publicly review their mistakes and triumphs of the year. No person, role, or situation may be untouched by the masquerade. By the end of a Gelede spectacle, the community will have reviewed and regenerated confidence in their lives.

This Gelede mask commemorates a Muslim or a Northerner who wears a cap with Islamic amulets delineated by the raised triangular packets. Amulets contain appropriate passages of the Koran, written out many times and then encased in leather. This strikingly convincing portrait of a diminutive bearded elder has been called an *alufa* or Muslim scholar and priest, but may just signify one who has adopted Islamic beliefs.

36. Mask (Epa)
Nigeria
Yoruba, 20th century
Wood, pigment, mirrored glass
H. 97.1 cm. (38 1/4″)
81.17.580

Performers wearing massive wood headdresses emerge from the forest each year in northeastern Yorubaland. Three examples of the masquerade best known as Epa are presented here. As a sequence, they provide an abbreviated but admirable impression of the Epa performances which incorporate many masks and last for days.

Epa masks are spoken of as "the great ones, the great ones of the family that are now dead." One feature they all share is a Janus helmet which fits over the dancer's head. On the helmet, the potlike *(ikoko)* head is always portrayed with fixed, almond-shaped eyes, broad mouth, and square ears. The *ikoko* face is that of the spirit of a deceased ancestor, while above, a superstructure of relatively realistic figures represent live characters, both human and animal. In this combination, the Epa mask truly becomes a vision of the living and the dead.

Each masked performer arrives and is greeted by praise names and dance rhythms that address the individual character represented in the Epa form. Oloko, the leopard, wearing a fresh green fringe of raffia fibers, is the first to arrive

from the forest. Villagers will salute this masquerader with a name such as "Master-of-the-Bush-About-the-Farm" or "Terror-to-All-Animals-Within-the-Bush." The leopard's qualities as a king of beasts and an agile hunter are verbally recognized.

The leopard atop the headdress attacks an antelope and curls his tail to support a snake being bitten by a bird. This arabesque interchange may relate to an order among the animals involved—the leopard with claws and teeth is more dangerous than the antelope with horns and teeth, who is more powerful than the bird with beak. Oloko's performance is strident and crucial to the entire Epa sequence. After running in to salute the elders who watch him carefully, Oloko must take a test. He must approach a mound of earth and jump onto it while maintaining his equilibrium with the weight of the Epa mask on his head. If successful, he brings an assurance of good luck to the farming and hunting for the year. If not, sacrifices must expiate his failure. Through this performance, the town determines whether their young men will have the strength to shoulder the responsibilities of the year ahead.

An aristocratic equestrian is the next Epa mask type to emerge from the forest. This Epa portrays a royal presence. He wears a tall conical hairstyle or headpiece which is often associated with royalty. Around his neck he wears a necklace of long coral beads, another symbol of status. As only an authoritative chief would, he carries a flywhisk which curves over his right shoulder.

Several other Epa masks were carved by a master of the Adechina School in the earlier part of this century. The succession of three faces—rider, horse, and ancestor—show an Adechina master's touch; the compressed volumes and finely delineated features of this example are Adechina hallmarks. Heavy-lidded eyes, full lips, and a sensitive rendering of the horseman catch one's attention. The horse's face is abbreviated to an extreme, but enlivened by a perfect circular chain of reins. The weighty, massive features of the *ikoko* head solidify the base. Fine linear detail is used throughout to focus points of interest.

Family members commissioned carvers to memorialize a deceased ancestor who deserved to be honored by the entire town. After the carving was completed, the owner might apply the coloration prior to a masquerade. Various natural pigments like ochre-colored ground stone, white powdered snail shells, and black ash would be used to make the paint. Considerable time and care was spent in painting this Epa. Broad reddish areas at the top and bottom are accented by the rider's complex patterning of minute dots and bands of yellow, white, and red color.

37. Mask (Epa)
Nigeria
Yoruba, Adechina School,
20th century
Wood, pigment
H. 122.5 cm. (48 1/4″)
81.17.578

38. Mask (Epa)
Bamgboye of Odo-Owa
Nigeria
Yoruba, 20th century
Wood, pigment
H. 118 cm. (46 1/2")
81.17.579

Bamgboye of Odo-Owa is credited with the creation of several monumental Epas with grandiose warriors. This is one, depicting a warrior who carries numerous weapons—a spear, a sword, and an enormous pistol in his right hand, a flywhisk and his horse's reins in his left. At either side, attendants with rifles as large as their own bodies bolster his military might. Musicians playing *dun-dun* drums and a deer-horn trumpet are also among his retinue. Together they document the loud and impressive cavalcade created by a conquering hero on horseback.

Whether this commander is being celebrated as a local hero or being critiqued as a foreign invader is unknown. His opulent trappings and communal supports may denote a warrior of honor. However, northeastern Yorubaland sustained a chain of catastrophic invasions that involved many raiders on horseback. Foreign invaders came from several directions to overrun Ekiti territory, while the Ekiti armies remained unmounted. Elements of northern-style clothing and horse trappings indicate that this may be a hostile warrior whose memory is being revived. The rimmed hat with large straps, the saddle with high pommel and cantle, and the horse's reins are all decorated with leather appliqué and tassels common to northern craftsmanship. Memorializing invaders may have aroused the Ekiti audience, enabling them to form plans for defense. Brilliant blue (Ricketts) paint has been applied to accent the decorative trappings of the entire entourage, adding yet another element to the intense complexity of the mask.

"Here is the lion. Acute analysis has snatched his essence.

"Here is the calm control of the beast, waiting with a quiet wide face, sudden narrow eyes and ears like sentinels. Only underneath all that poise and majesty, you find teeth."—KCW

During the proceedings of Kore, a senior inititation society, Bamana men watch the lion masquerade. Lion dancers move with distinctive calm and hold tall batons to maintain a measured pace. When the dancers jump they keep in synchronized step, always returning to a composed posture. Other animal masqueraders, like the hyena, may try to tease the lion into retaliation, but the lion's nobility never falters. After each challenge the lions advance slowly and look at their audience with quiet deliberation.

In this mask form, the Bamana commend the lion's restraint. They speak of the lion as doing nothing without meditation and reflection. Learning to make judicious use of one's strength is a tenet of Bamana belief. No animal is felt to illustrate this better than the lion whose awesome jaws are hidden from sight by a serene face. This potential force being held in check by an equanimity of mind is also commended in a Bamana praise salute:

Diara, Lion
Big bone-cruncher
Roaring in the thickest of thickets.
Stranger in the morning
Village chief by evening
You have curved the world like a
    sickle
You have straightened it out again
    into a road.
                (Zahan, 1963, pp. 137-38)

86

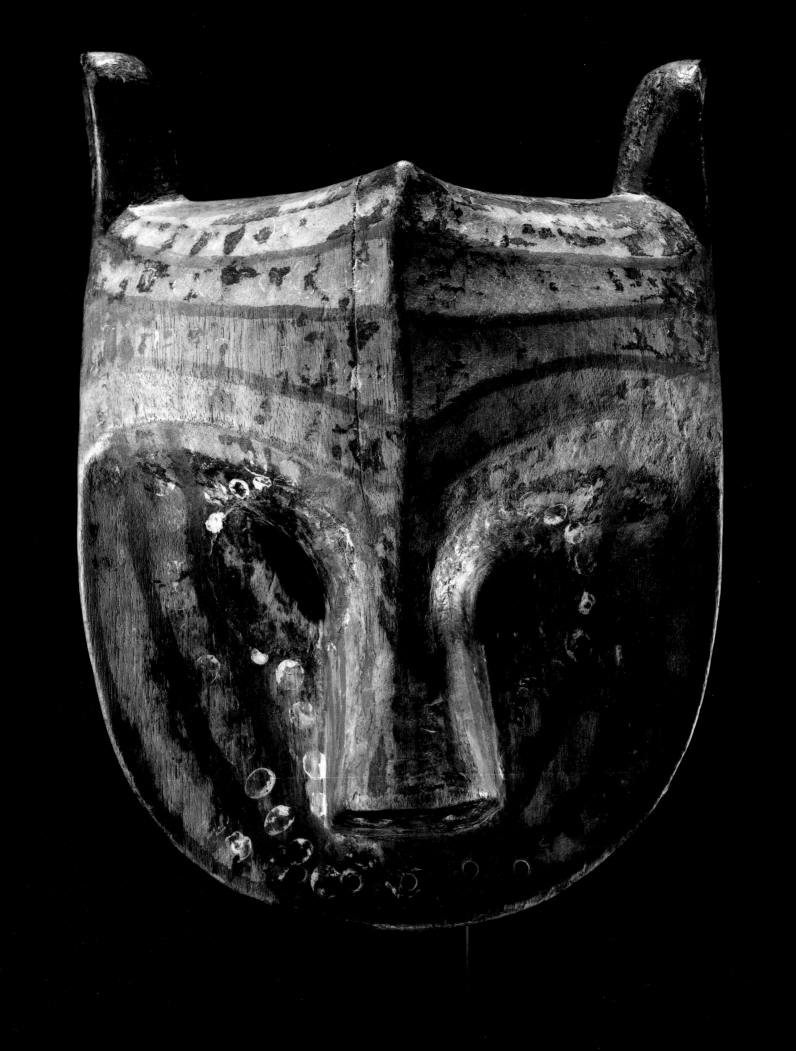

40. Mask *(hemba)*
Zaire
Suku, 19th-20th century
Wood, pigment, raffia
H. 49.2 cm. (19 3/8″)
81.17.909

A young Suku man was concealed beneath this helmet mask at a pivotal moment in his life. Just as he was leaving a period of training in an *nkanda* initiation camp, he donned the mask to introduce his new status. The mask acted as a shield to his remote and somewhat vulnerable new personality. Its protective value was enhanced by elders who activated it as a powerful charm, which no one could touch casually. Further charms were also placed inside the mask or attached to the shaggy fringe to ward off anyone who might try to harm the performer.

When the *nkanda* session closed, *hemba* masqueraders danced into Suku villages. Songs of mourning were customarily sung to accompany the mask at this time: "*Hemba* appeared anew ... as *hemba* cries, so *hemba* dances" (Bourgeois, 1979, p. 52). Tears are painted beneath the eyes of this mask, as seen in the vertical lines on the cheeks. It has been suggested that the *hemba* mask demonstrates an attachment to the Suku forebearers who guide *nkanda* initiates. Their allegience to *nkanda* teaching gives them both benevolent and dangerous talents which they must integrate with their adult life. Two knob projections at the top of this head are described as baskets for collecting food for which this character searches among the audience, partially in jest.

Earlier accounts describe eras when *hemba* masks were endowed with curative powers. Masqueraders were then known to present charms or medicines to aid in illness and ensure successful hunting. Currently, the *hemba* performer is predominantly an entertainer who celebrates the New Year, and dances during government visits and to please tourists. Within the last century, this *hemba* may have served as a potent safeguard at a time of change for a young adult, or as a lighthearted jester in a more contemporary context.

41. Helmet mask
Mali/Ivory Coast
Senufo, 19th century
Wood, metal
H. 128.3 cm. (50 1/2")
81.17.260

"It is an altar screen of iconography, numb soft signals long since recognized. Fastened there are chameleons, horse and rider, a pregnant woman pounding grain, and many cranes, solitary birds whose heavy beaks touch their chests to keep and recirculate strength.

"Buttressing the facade are the heads of a bush cow and a towering antelope with horns evolving into a female form. The pot she balances with a bird lid is a diviner's crucible where she carries chance and the future on her head. Her entire structure-shrine is a coordinated waiting."—KCW

A dancer wearing this large frieze fastened to his head was likely to have been a privileged sight. Senufo masks were once used in lessons preparing men for responsible adulthood. Lessons were conducted by elders of an association (Poro) in the midst of a sacred forest sanctuary *(sinzanga)*. Through Poro tutelage intricate interpretations of this composite icon would no doubt be possible; without it any explanation is a tenuous exercise. The repertoire of motifs does include many familiar Senufo images. Chameleons appear; their ability to transform their appearance involves them in many omens and taboos. A horse and rider lend status to the bottom tier, balancing two pregnant women pounding millet in a mortar on the other

side. The middle tier depicts a woman standing with staffs in a ceremonial stance while a possible funeral procession takes place on the opposite rung. Hornbills stand at the summit of the screen with square wings and beaks curving down to touch the full curves of their bellies. The phallic arc of the hornbill's beak meeting a bloated belly has been explained as a sign of physical and intellectual fertility. Survival requires such fecundity, just as society requires the regeneration of knowledge and skills.

The forefront of the mask features a woman astride an antelope head. She carries a calabash container on her head, perhaps of the type carried by diviners. Senufo women were often diviners and interpreters of relationships with supernatural worlds. Their presence was required to sanction the beginning of Poro activities. The narrow head and ringed horns of the antelope have also been added to this cumulative composition. For the Senufo, the antelope's role is that of a bush horse, admired for its speed, endurance, and beauty. These qualities augment those of the wild bush cow, another major symbol of power and magic, carved on the rear of the headdress.

Without field documentation these motifs may be identified, but barely interpreted. It remains the task of a Poro offical to maintain the knowledge coded into this mask and pass it on to the dedicated, worthy initiates.

42. Mask
Zaire
Luba, 19th-20th century
Wood, pigment
H. 48.3 cm. (19″)
81.17.868

Masterful balances are struck in this mask. The domed forehead creates a huge volume to the front, while a pair of sweeping hair extensions curve out to the back. Smooth, slightly dappled surfaces are held in check by a forehead crest and a beard/collar of braided and striped incisions. Added to these crisp lines, a sequence of red and white pigments form a polychrome striation of red, white, and black.

Comments beyond commending the visual force of this rare mask type are few. An intricately braided hairstyle was not an unusual men's fashion in Luba territory. A photograph of a Luba chief wearing a comparable horned coiffure illustrates this penchant for sculptured hair arrangements (Maes, 1939, p. 182). Two other similar masks are known; one in the Tervuren Museum was reportedly collected in 1889. What this face of many expressions was intended to portray has not been documented.

"His head is vast, his eyes are deep in folds, squinting through wrinkled layers.... Change the angle of his head and he will change. The eyes die, dry up and see nothing. The laugh becomes the cackle of cynicism. Bitter, aggressive, the face holds you at a distance as it ridicules."—KCW

43. Mask *(kifwebe)*
Zaire
Luba, prior to 1913
Wood, raffia, bark, pigment, twine
H. 92.1 cm. (36 1/4")
81.17.869

In 1913 Father Colle, a Belgian missionary, published his notes about *kifwebe* masks and included one field photograph. The photograph was later lauded as it "shows a stunning example of what has come to epitomize the Baluba Kifwebe mask style" (Merriam, 1978, p. 60). Close examination reveals that this mask is the very one photographed by Colle. As such, it may be securely dated prior to 1913.

Father Colle's report is also valuable for its brief description of the *kifwebe* appearance:

There is a dance where the dancers are dressed in a special costume: on the arms and legs a sort of sack made of tree bark, at the waist skins, at the neck an immense collar of fiber, suspended from a ring on the head a large mask of wood. They generally dance in pairs; one represents a male spirit, the other a female spirit, the latter recognizable by the larger dimensions of the helmet. Each has in hand a large club made of "ambach wood," lighter than cork. Their dance is done in honor of certain spirits.

(Colle, 1913, pp.676-77)

Seventy years later, many other Luba *kifwebe* have been collected, but further documentation has not been accumulated.

(The *kifwebe* mask will not be included in the national tour of the exhibition.)

"Like a stone thrown into water the lines of this old face dilate in wakening circles. It grows like a huge moon in the mind. Pursed, closed, the vast inhuman countenance claims its territories. Those heavy-lidded eyes are not asleep but surreptitiously scan. The mouth muses. The dome obtrudes. The center pivots the whirlpools. Alone, old, the hold of its enormous power pours."

—KCW

Ga WreeWree is a reminder that masks were not just wooden face coverings, but entire ensembles and complete characters. This Dan mask begins with a weathered face with slit horizontal eyes and a forehead ridge. Such narrow eyes designate that this is a female mask of discreet countenance, quite unlike male masks that have bulging globular eyes. Accoutrements subsume the wooden section with layers of a headdress and collar. Alternating red and blue beads outline the chin; a row of brass bells suspended from them chime with the movement of the performer. Above, a dense band of cowrie shells adds an element of wealth and prestige. Crowning these strands is a fan of bone and metal hairpins, usually worn by women, but given to the masquerader over the years. A section of red netting then leads to a towering conical extension at the back of the head. A striped shawl and a wide skirt of raffia fiber completed the masquerader's costume. The costumed character's movements, an accompanying orchestra, and songs and dialogues informed the Dan audience which specific spirit was inhabiting the mask and arriving with such animation.

Due to an acute resemblance with a documented field study, this Dan mask has been called Ga WreeWree, Final-Decision-Maker, Dense Forest. When an important dispute was about to be heard, Ga WreeWree appeared with attendants and sat to hear the case. Presiding in a costume that removed her from the realm of men and gave her utmost authority, she listened to the defendant and plaintiff. When she had reached a decision, Ga WreeWree spoke in a disguised falsetto voice and thereby completed the mystic status of a divine female judge who came from the forest.

The slinking posture of a leopard with its predatory jaws wide open is depicted in an unusual medium. Soft sculpture is used to suggest the union of a fearless feline and a python. Wood and sisal are shaped into a substructure covered with blue felt. White, blue, and pink seed beads are sewn on in units of small triangles meant to represent the spots, teeth, and round ears of the leopard.

Leopard/pythons were selected for sculptural treatment for several reasons. In the Bamileke hierarchy, the leopard, elephant, and python were held in highest repute. The leopard above all was known to be master of his own environment, and was able to transform himself into human forms. A desirable symbol of authority, the leopard's use was restricted to the king (Fon) and those who had earned access to its implied prestige. Only men of considerable means who paid fees to the Fon and acted in accordance with societal rules were able to don this ornate mask form. In return for this right, the Elephant Society members were expected to defend the Fon's position as the master of the human environment. During times of crisis, death, succession, and ancestor cult/ fertility ceremonies, the members danced to validate the Fon's eminence.

Leopard and elephant masks performed jointly. Dancers were dressed in several layers of cloth, beaded vests, and wore rattles on their ankles. Their movements, accompanied by a single drum and gong while each dancer simultaneously emitted a tuneless whistle, have been described as slow and lurching. Such artistic gatherings were held every other year for society assemblies and to validate ceremonies involving the Fon.

"Gloomy architectonic vaults invade this head. The nose and looming structural eyebrows hold heavy caverns. There never was a mouth, only this vast glance.

"He harrows an audience ... like a minotaur. ... He knows the role, the heavy hollow sounds, the thuds, whirls of rage, blurts of intimidation, the lunge that terrifies. He gathers hate, disease, all evil into a single episode ... to protect a village by exorcising all possible threats, draining their wrongs for the coming year. He clears the air."—KCW

When collected in the Ivindo Basin area of Gabon, this mask called Mbuto was witnessed in an evening performance.

The mask came out, aggressively hurling arrows and spears into the crowd. The crowd in turn cajoled him, calling him "dear grandfather" and gently urged him into peace and calm. Gradually, as the dance progressed, the angle of the mask tipped forward and the arrows fell less far, finally hitting the ground only five feet away.

(Katherine White's files)

Other published accounts of Kota masks neither collaborate nor clarify the use and appearance of this mask form. One illustration of a similar mask with a raffia fringe being attended by men and women in the Kwele area is said to serve in initiation rituals called *satsi*.

A resounding set of curves and counteracting arched blades dominate the face. Traces of spotted white paint cover the upper half of the mask, while the lower shows signs of having been coated with black. Recent observers credit missionary activity, colonial forced labor practices, and the ravaging of wood which naturally occurs in the equatorial forest with the disappearance of many renowned Kota art forms.

100

46. Mask (Mbuto)
Gabon
Kota, 19th-20th century
Wood, traces of pigment and fiber
H. 68 cm. (26 3/4″)
81.17.785

47. Mask (Mabu), Kwifon Society
Wum Division, Cameroon
Wum, 19th century
Wood
H. 37.8 cm. (14 7/8″)
81.17.699

Mabu, the Running Mask of the Kwifon, is the forewarning of an imperious group of men on the move. He arrives wearing a spiky cloak of multiple layers of feathers and a fiber hood to conceal his face. As he moves through town, his mask is tilted up over his forehead so that the face looks skyward. A whistle is blown to announce the sight to come, which women and children are forbidden to see. They are given enough time to leave in order to hide from the group following Mabu. Once Mabu has had a chance to "clear the way and cleanse the air," other members of the Kwifon Society make their entrance. The Kwifon Society is drawn from high ranking lineages and wields considerable control over the regulation of Wum life. In restricted meetings, this society is responsible for making decisions with the Fon regarding law and order. It has informants everywhere, as expressed in the Wum proverb "Every blade of grass is Kwifon's eyes and ears" (Clement, 1965, p. 157). If an infraction or crime is committed, Kwifon members know quickly and set out at night in masked anonymity to make arrests. Mabu is their public spokesman. He runs ahead, alerting everyone of the society's imminent actions. His face is well suited to an intimidating role, with eyes deeply set and vestigial in form beneath a massive overhanging brow. Sharp ridges of hair are echoed by a bristling fence of teeth.

This example was kept in the roof storage of a royal compound, where it was said to have been retired around 1900.

48. Crocodile headdress
Nigeria/Cameroon
Cross River, Ekoi,
19th-20th century
Wood, skin, basketry
W. 97.8 cm. (38 1/2")
81.17.507

"From a water-woven land come creatures of convoluted imagination. They know where the power lies—in essences of female and reptile. From slime, disease, insects, the sludge of earth and river come composite formations as natural as oil. It's a subterfuge, the making of articulate spirit and lucrative heat."—KCW

This mask form is thought to combine a crocodile face with the elaborate spiral coiffure of a young woman. They unite on a basketry base to provide an image of the Cross River belief in transformation and beauty/beast dualities. Joining a crocodile face to a female hairstyle may derive from the Cross River concept of animal "familiars." Persons with extraordinary abilities or unusual inclinations could attribute their actions to the persuading force of an animal who sought them out. Certain animals could have a helpful and enhancing nature, but others could be dangerous and destructive. Crocodiles are classified as the latter type and may serve as agents of witchcraft. Whether this mask relates to a female anti-witchcraft association or a royal protection cult is not known.

The mask is covered by animal skin and darkened with a natural dark brown stain. A hole in the forehead probably once held a crown. It would have been worn on top of the head with a cloth gown that covered the dancer's entire body.

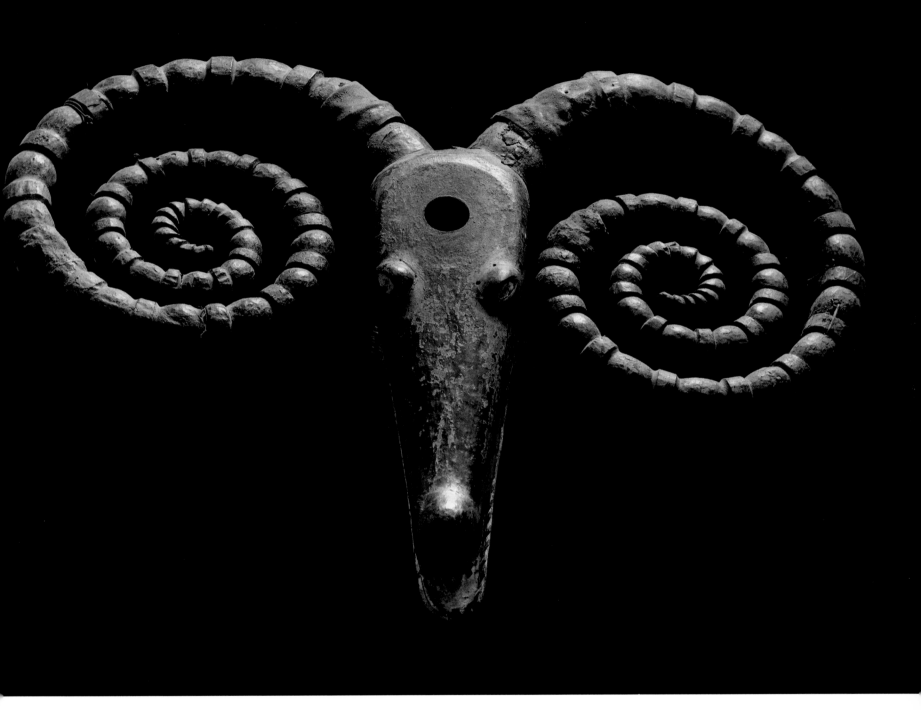

49. Three-faced helmet mask
Akparabong area, Nigeria
Ejagham, late 19th century
Wood, skin, pigment
H. 38.4 cm. (15 1/8")
81.17.506

In a tactile tour de force, this mask uses animal skin stretched over a wooden core. First carved with features designed to project from beneath the skin covering, the sculptor put special emphasis on projecting eyebrows, lips, and a sharp jaw line. Fresh skin was then dehaired but not cleaned on the flesh side, and pressed over the wood, sewn with string, and left to dry. The fatty particles of the skin became a natural adhesive, adhering the skin to the wood. Palm oil was later applied to restore suppleness to the skin and give it a gleaming finish before a performance.

Dark pigment distinguishes the massive male face from the two yellowish female faces, whose foreheads have also been marked to emulate facial tatoos or painting found on young women. Further realistic details are the inserted teeth which show a traditional deformation of the central incisors.

Worn over the head and cupped around the shoulders at the curving sides, this mask was present at the initations and funerals of members of warrior associations. An image of dual vision—dark and light, male and female, evil and good—it could have fittingly served as an emblem for the warriors' powerful status and pervasive knowledge. Associations were responsible for maintaining their own artworks and devised effective means of conservation to preserve their skin masks. For storage, the masks were wrapped in bark cloth or leaves and suspended from the ceiling near a cooking fire, where they were best protected from insects, rodents, and fungal attacks. This example is thought to be the work of Takim Eyuk, who carved several similar examples around the turn of the century.

"A kaleidoscope of faces swings around to impale us. Two of them are unutterably feminine. They intone poems of counterpointed privacy on xylophones of bamboo teeth. Tight skin pulls at the shrill black lines carving the faces into programmed ceremony. A huge black face anchors. His sounds are hard and veined with ore. The massive frontal lobe looms through its brittle membrane as ominously as a snake seeking to shed its skin.

"Who are these three?"—KCW

50. Basinjom mask and gown
Upper Cross River, Cameroon,
Ejagham, 20th century
Cloth, wood, feathers, porcupine
quills, mirrors, herbs, raffia,
cowrie shells, rattle, eggshell,
knife, genet cat skin
H. 216 cm. (irregular) (85″)
81.17.1977

110

"All elements join. The sea in the cowrie shells. The land and rivers in the mud crowding his head. The birds in his crown feathers. Animals in the skin of a genet cat hanging before him. Plants in the huge seed clutched between his teeth, or the tiny rim of grass worn as a necklace. Even man does not escape: the cloth of the gown has our sewing.

"He sags under the antennae, like a mine sweeper, like a seer, he intrudes into all dimensions. Dimmed mirrored eyes obtrude, the third one secreted in the back of the head devastates all. At the shake of his rattle we congeal." — KCW

Basinjom wages artistic battles. Uniting the skills of a detective and a diviner, he seeks out the evil forces in Banyang communities. Whenever he finds signs of extreme selfishness or deceit, he does his best to expose them. Through Basinjom, the Banyang have a creative way of denouncing disruptive personalities.

Banyang beliefs speak of persons who have double identities. Those who exhibit negative behavior may be supporting an animal counterpart that has become attached to a human host. Harmful counterparts such as the owl, python, and bush pig are the targets for Basinjom's attack. Their presence may persuade a person to act irresponsibly or to think negatively. Duplicity and selfish behavior are perceived as being common human problems which Basinjom can conceptually confront.

Through an initiate's eyes, the Basinjom costume is seen as a composition of animal and man-made referents. From the top, there are feathers from a blue war bird to signify strength. Mirrored eyes enable Basinjom's vision to penetrate into the secret realms of hidden thoughts. A rattle enables him to hear the sound that evil makes. The snout of a crocodile adds the impact of a reptile on the prowl. The head

is embedded with a mixture of clay, herbs, and medicines to protect the performer from evil. A genet cat skin puts the ferocious image of a predator out in front like a shield. Raffia bristles at the hems to bring a raw bush energy into place. Dark indigo and black cloth are chosen to foil the vision of evildoers.

Prior to adopting Basinjom's character, an initiate is primed with a solution of tulip tree resin, and palm wine is dropped and sprayed into his eyes. He then takes on Basinjom's spirit, is quickly dressed in this costume, and sets out with a small orchestra and army at his side. Raising the front of the gown, Basinjom seemingly glides by, taking rapid, minute steps as he swirls about town. Sweeping through compounds, he stalks evil in the audience of villagers. When he finds a suspect, he stops, shakes, and recites the misdeeds or nasty words of the person in question. Humiliated publicly, the malcontent is forced to confess.

Basinjom is known to appear at any time, and may suprise a village with an unexpected visit. His talent for identifying and artistically assaulting negative personalities is aptly remembered in this arsenal of costume and clairvoyant iconography.

51. Mask, Ekpo Society
Calabar Province, Nigeria
Ibibio, 20th century
Wood
H. 31.4 cm. (12 3/8″)
81.17.514

Ravaged and distorted faces are seen annually in Ekpo masquerades. Their repulsiveness is enhanced by a masquerader who coats his body with charcoal and oil and wears shaggy, dishevelled rags and raffia fibers. Through deliberate ugliness, Ekpo ceremonies provide a review of both medical and moral problems in Ibibio life.

This mask, with its nose twisted into a pretzel shape, alludes to a deformation caused by gangosa. A vitamin deficiency disease, gangosa can destroy nasal membranes and results in severe disfigurement. Masks commemorate and often exaggerate the disease as an attribute of certain *ekpo*, those spirits or ghosts who have died violent deaths and may try to bring catastrophes to their home village. Ekpo performers arrive in a state of agitation, shaking with rage. Their repugnant appearance is matched by their destructive behavior. Lurching around the village, the Ekpo performer rushes about in erratic movements, threatens onlookers with dangerous knives, ransacks property, and shoots arrows at women. In several ways, the Ekpo vision epitomizes ugliness and the traits detrimental to Ibibio life. In this live demonstration the threat of disfiguring disease is equated with improper behavior.

These masqueraders were also agents from the Ekpo Society who considered what to do about crimes committed during the year. They could inflict punishments in an effort to maintain social order. During an annual season Ekpo maskers performed for male initiates, but allowed women to observe only two public performances a year.

52. Great Mother mask (Iyanla)
Nigeria
Yoruba, 20th century
Wood, incrustations, feathers
H. 39 cm. (15 3/8″)
81.17.586

"This is mute force. It will hypnotize. The eyes are huge, they bulge in craters of the face. The cheeks are heavy, the mouth shuts upon its words. By day there's nothing, cataracts of dull gray scale crust the eyes, the narrow shiny trails of old blood sacrifices pour over the forehead like speeding black rain. The face rests. By dark, the face illuminates, glows. Round and round the shapes pour out, gathering all into its intelligence, focusing, arousing, pugnacious. Never evil, yet it lives in death, sleeping in a trance of power."—KCW

Iyanla is an image submerged in secrecy. Most of the year it is shrouded by a spotless white cloth in a darkened white shrine. Only one or two cult leaders may see it in order to present offerings of food that accumulate on the extension plank of the mask. Once a year, Iyanla enters a Yoruba town to perform in total darkness. No lights are allowed to illuminate her face and elders escort her in a tight circle to limit the audience's view. Even in this performance, the mask is covered by a long white cloth, trailing to the ground. The masker must remain crouched, to support the mask in a horizontal position. Slowly, Iyanla proceeds through town while songs and drum rhythms accompany her. As a mask, the Iyanla image is starkly defined. Enormous eyes dominate a face with a swollen forehead. It is said that the heads of persons in the midst of possession swell with spiritual presence. Iyanla's face derives from such intense inner power. A beard is added beneath, implying the distinction of an elder whose wisdom and commanding status become a part of the mask.

Tributes paid to the Great Mother mask address a Yoruba concern for the covert abilities of women. Just as Iyanla is a concealed face of implied force, so an entire side of the feminine mind remains unknown. A female exterior may appear calm just at the point when a strong concentration of spiritual force is present. If not assuaged and recognized, the female may become unpredictably malicious, transform into a nocturnal creature, and seek to attack those who have offended her. The Yoruba recognize this potential spiritual power in women and visualize it in the elusive Iyanla.

In return for this attention, Iyanla becomes "the nightwatch for the town" (Drewal and Drewal, 1983, p. 77). Many medicines are deposited on the mask when positioned in a shrine. Sacred ingredients soak into the wood, enabling her to serve well as the guardian of the community. Although these medicines are invisible, their residue accumulates on the mask and contributes to its awesome aura.

115

53. Mask
Liberia/Ivory Coast
Wee, 20th century
Wood, raffia, cloth, teeth, horn,
feathers, hair, natural fiber cord,
cowrie shells
H. 81 cm. (32″)
81.17.193

"He festers a welter of horns and shell and eyes, teeth protruding, hairs sprouting, hanging, glaring. Dense and hideous.

"He is dark and heavy but also fragile. How can anything so mis-shapen be so benign? Not quite the devil's advocate, yet the role of terror is a duty here. He is extreme so that others may feel the soothing warmth of safety."

—KCW

Like a magnet for terror, this face has drawn to it a mass of raw and ragged emblems of evil. To see it is a frightful encounter with the spirits that roam the bush or forest outside the controlled existence of villages and towns.

When unexplained calamities or social tensions arise, this mask may make an appearance. Its gruesome strength enables the masquerader to proceed through a village and chase away the witches that brought the potential for epidemics or drought that could disrupt the community. All the suggestions of wild animalistic forces are drawn to the face to attain an image that can then combat forces threatening village life. It emanates from a bumpy red core and then sprouts out in several directions with animal parts—antelope horns, teeth, black hair and fur.

Through this metaphor of the untamed, arbitrary animalistic force of the forest, the village population is able to visualize its need to act quite the opposite—orderly, productive, and civilized.

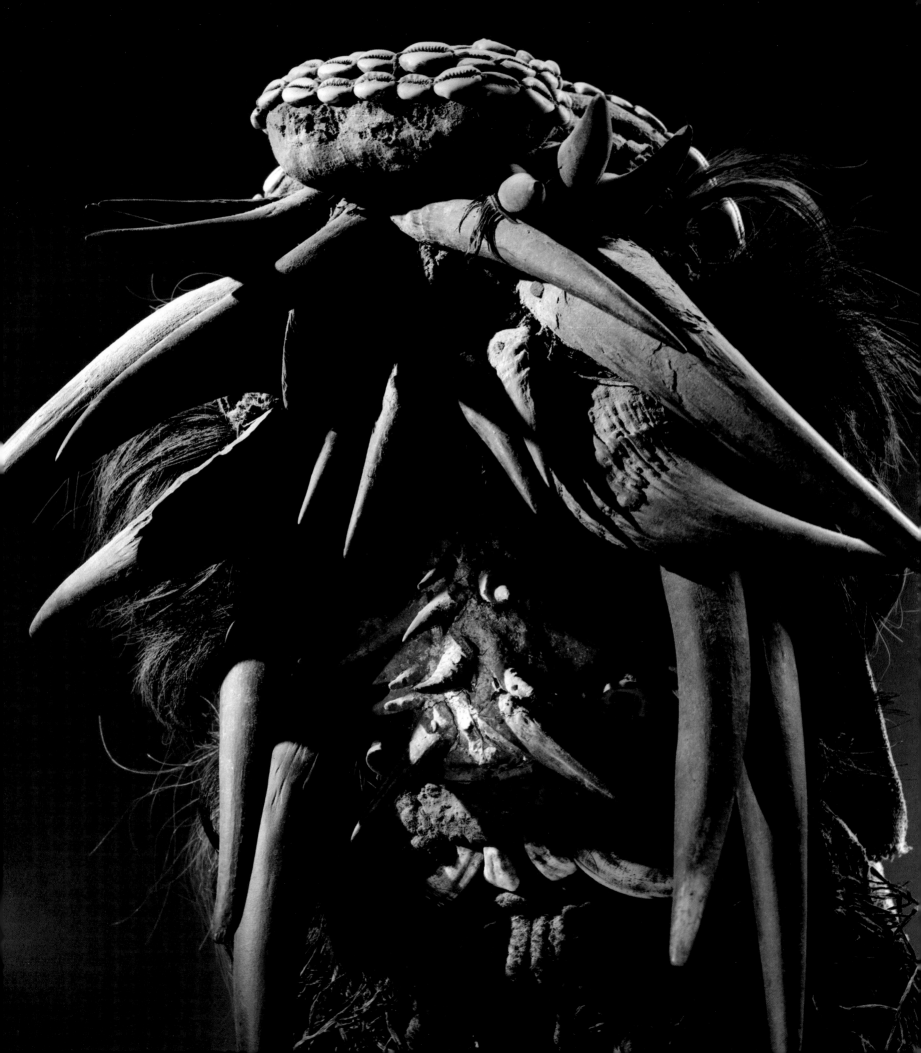

BIBLIOGRAPHY

Katherine White's collection is surrounded by a host of resources. Her documentation cards, slide archives, and library reflect her continual pursuit of comparative artwork and scholarly opinion. The catalogues previously published on the collection—*African Tribal Images*, by William Fagg, and *African Art in Motion: Icon and Act*, by Robert Farris Thompson—establish a base of information and insight. Updating these resources has been the task of Pam McClusky, Norman Skougstad, Linda Knudsen, and Annica Wambaugh. Their efforts have been aided by written and verbal communications from Henry and Margaret Drewal, William Fagg, Keith Nicklin, John Pemberton III, Jill Salmons, Gilbert Schneider, Roy Sieber, Robert Farris Thompson, and Susan Vogel.

The entries in this catalogue merely summarize a widening body of literature on the artistry of Africa. References cited in the text and other sources are listed here to encourage the reader's further interest.

References Cited

Abimbola, W. *Ifa Divination Poetry*. New York: Nok Publishers, Ltd., 1977.

Bascom, William. *Ifa Divination: Communication between Gods and Men in West Africa*. Bloomington: Indiana University Press, 1969.

Basden, G. T. *Among the Ibos of Nigeria*. London: Seeley Service and Co. Ltd., 1921.

Beier, Ulli. *Yoruba Poetry: An Anthology of Traditional Poems*. London: Cambridge University Press, 1970.

Ben-Amos, Paula. *The Art of Benin*. London: Thames and Hudson, 1980.

_____, ed. *The Art of Power/The Power of Art: Studies in Benin Iconography*. Los Angeles: Museum of Cultural History, University of California, 1983.

Bourgeois, Arthur P. *Nkanda Related Sculpture of the Yaka and Suku of Southwestern Zaire*. Ann Arbor, Mich.: University Microfilms, 1979.

Clement, Njob. "Lore and Learning in Mankon Tongue, Bamenda West Cameroon," *Abbia* (Yaounde, Cameroon), 9-10 (1965): 157.

Colle, P. *Les Baluba*. Collection de Monographies Ethnographiques, 10, 11. Brussels: Albert deWit, 1913.

Delano, Isaac O. *Owe L'Esin Oro: Yoruba Proverbs*. Ibadan, Nigeria: Oxford University Press, 1966.

Drewal, Henry J., and Margaret Thompson Drewal. *Gelede: Art and Dance Among the Yoruba*. Bloomington: Indiana University Press, 1983.

Egudu, Romanus, and Donatus Nwoga. *Igbo Traditional Verse*. London: Heinemann, 1973.

Fischer, Eberhard, and Hans Himmelheber. *Die Kunst der Dan*. Zurich: Rietberg Museum, 1976.

Foss, Wilson Perkins. "The Arts of the Urhobo Peoples of Southern Nigeria." Ph.D. Diss., Yale University, 1976.

Laurenty, J. S. "Les Cordophones du Congo Belge et du Ruandi-Urundi," in *Annales du Museé Royal du Congo Belge*, N.S. in 4, Sciences de l'Homme, (Tervuren, Belgium) 2 (1960): 182.

Maes, J. "Kabila—en Grafbeelden uit Kongo," in *Annales du Museé Royal du Congo Belge*, Ethnographie Serie 6, (Tervuren, Belgium) 2, no.3 (1939): 182.

Merriam, Alan P. "Kifwebe and Other Masked and Unmasked Societies Among the Basongye," *Africa-Tervuren*, 24 (1978): 3, 4.

Roy, Christopher. *Mossi Masks and Crests*. Ann Arbor, Mich.: University Microfilms, 1979.

Schweeger-Hefel, A.M. *Masken und Mythen: Sozial Strukturen des Nyonyosi und Sikomse aus Obervolta*. Vienna: Schendl Verlag, 1980.

Vergiat, A. M. *Les Rites Secrets des Primitifs de l'Oubangui*. Paris: Payot, 1951.

Williams, Denis. *Icon and Image: A Study of Sacred and Secular Forms of African Classical Art*. New York: New York University Press, 1974.

Zahan, Dominique. *La Dialectique du Verbe chez les Bambara*. Paris-La Haye: Mouton and Co., 1963.

_____. *Antilopes du Soleil: Arts et Rites Agraires d'Afrique Noire*. Vienna: Edition A. Schendl, 1980.

Catalogues

Achter Spiegels: Spiegel-enspijker-beelden uit Neder-Kongo. Berg-en-dal, Netherlands: Afrike Museum, 1981.

Arnett, William, and Marcilene K. Wittmer. *Three Rivers of Nigeria*. Atlanta: The High Museum of Art, 1978.

Blier, Suzanne. *Beauty and the Beast*. New York: Kahan Gallery, 1978.

_____. *Africa's Cross River*. New York: Kahan Gallery, 1980.

Cole, Herbert M., and Doran H. Ross. *The Arts of Ghana*. Los Angeles: Museum of Cultural History, University of California, 1977.

119

Drewal, Henry J. *Traditional Art of the Nigerian Peoples.* Washington, D.C.: Museum of African Art, 1977.

_____. *African Artistry: Technique and Aesthetics in Yoruba Sculpture.* Atlanta: The High Museum of Art, 1980.

Fagg, William. "Tribal Art," *Christie's* (London), July 13, 1977.

_____. *African Majesty from Grassland and the Forest.* Toronto: Art Gallery of Ontario, 1981.

Fagg, William, and John Pemberton III. *Yoruba Sculpture of West Africa.* New York: Alfred A. Knopf, 1982.

Fry, Jacqueline, ed. *Twenty-Five African Sculptures.* Ottawa: National Gallery of Canada, 1978.

Gebauer, Paul. *Art of Cameroon.* Portland, Oreg.: Portland Art Museum, 1979.

Goldwater, Robert. *Senufo Sculpture from West Africa.* New York: Museum of Primitive Art, 1964.

High-Wasikhongo, Freida. *Traditional African Art: A Female Focus.* Madison: Elvehjem Museum of Art, University of Wisconsin, 1981.

Imperato, Pascal James. *Dogon Cliff-Dwellers.* New York: Kahan Gallery, 1978.

Koloss, Han-Joachim. *Kamerun Könige Masken Feste.* Stuttgart: Instituts fur Auslandsbeziehungen, Stuttgart, and Linden Museum, 1977.

Laude, Jean. *African Art of the Dogon.* New York: Brooklyn Museum, 1973.

New York University. Grey Art Gallery. *Images of Power: Art of the Royal Court of Benin.* New York: New York University, 1981.

Nicklin, Keith. *Guide to the National Museum, Oron.* Lagos, Nigeria: Nigerian Federal Department of Antiquities, 1977.

Northern, Tamara. *Royal Art of Cameroon.* Hanover, New Hampshire: Hopkins Center Art Galleries, Dartmouth, 1973.

_____. *The Sign of the Leopard, Beaded Art of Cameroon.* Storrs, Conn.: The William Benton Museum of Art, University of Connecticut, 1975.

Rubin, Arnold. *Figurative Sculptures of the Niger River Delta.* Los Angeles: Gallery K., 1976.

Siegmann, William, and Cynthia Schmidt. *Rock of the Ancestors: Namoa Koni.* Suacoco, Liberia: Cuttington College, 1977.

Sotheby Parke Bernet and Co. *Catalogue of a Collection of Benin Works of Art.* London: Sotheby Parke Bernet, June 16, 1980.

Thompson, Robert Farris. *Black Gods and Kings: Yoruba Art at UCLA.* Los Angeles: University of California, 1971.

Vevers, T. *Interaction: Art Styles of the Benue River Valley.* West Lafayette: Gallery II, Purdue University, 1974.

Vogel, Susan M., ed. *For Spirits and Kings: African Art from the Paul Tishman Collection.* New York: The Metropolitan Museum of Art, 1981.

Books

Awolain, J. Omosade. *Yoruba Beliefs and Sacrificial Rites.* London: Longman Group Ltd., 1979.

Babalola, S. A. *The Content and Form of Yoruba Ijala.* Oxford: Clarendon Press, 1966.

Barnes, Sandra T. *Ogun: Old God for a New Age.* Philadelphia: Institute for the Study of Human Issues, 1980.

Basden, G. T. *Niger Ibos.* London: Frank Cass and Co., Ltd., 1938.

Bastin, Marie-Louise. *La Sculpture Tshokwe.* Paris: Alain et Francoise Chaffin, 1982.

Bellis, James O. *The Place of Pots in Akan Funerary Custom.* Bloomington: African Studies Program, Indiana University, 1982.

Brain, Robert, and Adam Pollock. *Bangwa Funerary Sculpture.* London: Gerald Duckworth and Co., Ltd., 1971.

Carroll, Kevin. *Yoruba Religious Carving.* New York: Praeger, 1966.

Cornet, Joseph. *Art of Africa.* London: Phaidon Press, 1971.

Dark, Philip J. C. *An Introduction to Benin Art and Technology.* Oxford: Clarendon Press, 1973.

Glaze, Anita J. *Art and Death in a Senufo Village.* Bloomington: Indiana University Press, 1981.

Grunne, Bernard de. *Terres Cuites Anciennes de l'Ouest Africain.* Louvain-la-Neuve: Institut Superieur d'Archeologie et d'Histoire de l'Art, 1980.

Janzen, John. *The Quest for Therapy in Lower Zaire.* Berkeley: University of California Press, 1978.

Law, Robin. *The Horse in West African History.* London: Oxford University Press, 1980.

Lawal, Babatunde. *Yoruba Sango Sculpture in Historical Retrospect.* Ann Arbor, Mich.: University Microfilms, 1970.

Maes, J. *Aniota-Kifwebe.* Antwerp: De Sikkel, 1924.

Moal, Guy Le. *Les Bobo, Nature et Fonction des Masques.* Paris: ORSTOM, 1980.

Neyt, François. *Traditional Arts and History of Zaire.* Brussels: Societe d'Arts Primitifs, 1981.

Pelton, Robert. *The Trickster in West Africa.* Berkeley: University of California Press, 1983.

Perrois, Louis. *Arts du Gabon.* Arts d'Afrique Noire. Paris: Arnouville and ORSTOM, 1979.

Rattray, R. S. *Religion and Art in Ashanti.* Oxford: Clarendon Press, 1927.

Ritzenthaler, Robert, and Pat Ritzenthaler. *Cameroons Village.* Milwaukee Public Museum, Publications in Anthropology, no. 8. Milwaukee: North American Press, 1962.

Ruel, Malcolm. *Leopards and Leaders-A Constitutional Politics among a Cross River People.* London and New York: Tavistock Publications, 1969.

Schwab, George. *Tribes of the Liberian Hinterland.* Peabody Museum Papers, no. 31. Cambridge: Peabody Museum, 1947.

Schwartz, Nancy Beth A. *Mambilla—Art and Material Culture.* Milwaukee: Milwaukee Public Museum, 1975.

Starkweather, Frank. *Traditional Igbo Art.* Ann Arbor, Mich.: University of Michigan, 1966.

Thompson, Robert Farris. *Flash of the Spirit.* New York: Random House, 1983.

Vjard, Rene. *Les Gueres: Peuple de la Forêt.* Paris: Société d' Editions, 1934.

Zahan, Dominique. *Sociétiés d'Initiation Bambara: Le N'domo, le Kore.* Paris: Mouton and Co., 1960.

Articles

Ben-Amos, Paula. "Man and Animals in Benin Art," *Man*, 11 (1979): 243-52.

Clarke, J. D. "Three Yoruba Fertility Ceremonies," *Journal of the Royal Anthropological Institute*, 74 (1944): 91-96.

Drewal, Henry J. "Art and the Perception of Women in Yoruba Culture," *Cahiers d'Etudes Africaines*, 17 (1977): 545-67.

Fernandez, James W. "Principles of Opposition and Vitality in Fang Aesthetics," *Journal of Aesthetics and Art Criticism*, 25, no.1 (1966): 53-64.

Fischer, Eberhard. "Dan Forest Spirits: Masks in Dan Villages," *African Arts*, 11, no. 2 (1978): 16-23, 94.

Flam, Jack D. "The Symbolic Structure of Baluba Caryatid Stools," *African Arts*, 4, no. 2 (1971): 54-59, 80.

Foss, Wilson Perkins. "Images of Aggression: Ivwri Sculpture of the Urhobo," in *African Images: Essays in African Iconology*, edited by Daniel McCall and Edna Bay. New York: African Publishing Co., 1975.

Fry, Phillip. "Essai sur la Statuaire Mumuye," *Objets et Mondes*, 10, no. 1 (1970): 3-27.

Glaze, Anita J. "Woman Power and Art in a Senufo Village," *African Arts*, 8, no. 3 (1975): 24-29, 64-90.

Imperato, Pascal James. "The Dance of the Tyi Wara," *African Arts*, 4, no. 3 (1970): 8-13, 71-80.

_____. "Last Dances of the Bambara," *Natural History*, 84 (1975): 62-71.

Jeffreys, M. D. W. "The Nyama Society of the Ibibio Women," *African Studies*, 15, no. 4 (1956): 15-28.

Kaberry, P. M., and E. M. Chilver. "The Kingdom of Kom in West Cameroon," in *West African Kingdoms in the Nineteenth Century*, edited by D. Forde and P. M. Kaberry. London: International African Institute, 1967.

Kauenhoven-Janzen, Reinhild. "Chokwe Thrones," *African Arts*, 14, no. 3 (1981): 69-74.

Lantum, D. N. "Superstition," *Abbia* (Yaounde, Cameroon), 21 (1969): 147-61.

Lawal, Babatunde. "New Light on Gelede," *African Arts*, 11, no. 21 (1978): 65-70, 94.

McCall, Daniel F. "The Hornbill and Analagous Forms in West African Sculpture," in *African Images: Essays in African Iconology*, edited by D. McCall and Edna G. Bay. New York: Africana Publishing Co., 1975.

McCulloch, Merran. "Tikar," in *Peoples of the Central Cameroons, Western Africa Part 9, Ethnographic Survey of Africa*, edited by Daryll Forde. London: International African Institute, 1954.

McGaffey, Wyatt. "Fetishism Revisited: Kongo Nkisi in Sociological Perspective," *Africa*, 47, no. 2 (1977): 172-84.

Malcolm, L. W. G. "Notes on the Ancestral Cult Ceremonies of the Eyap, Central Cameroons," *The Journal of the Royal Anthropological Institute of Great Britain and Ireland*, 55 (1935): 373-405.

Messenger, John C. "The Carver in Anang Society," in *The Traditional Artist in African Society*, edited by Warren d'Azevedo. Bloomington: Indiana University Press, 1973.

Murray, Kenneth C. "Ekpu: The Ancestor Figures of Oron, Southern Nigeria," *Burlington Magazine* (1947): 310-14.

_____. "Ogbom," *The Nigerian Field*, 10, (1941): 127-131.

Nicklin, Keith. "Nigerian Skin-Covered Masks," *African Arts*, 7, no. 3 (1974): 8-15, 67-68, 92.

Nsugbe, P. O. "Oron Ekpu Figures," *Nigeria Magazine*, 71 (1961): 356-63.

Ojo, J. R. O. "The Symbolism and Significance of Epa-type Masquerade Headpieces," *Man*, 13 (1978): 455-70.

Pemberton, John, III. "Eshu-Elegba: The Yoruba Trickster God," *African Arts*, 9, no. 1 (1975): 20-27, 66-70, 90-92.

_____. "Sacred Kingship and the Violent God: The Worship of Ogun among the Yoruba," *Berkshire Review*, 14 (1979): 85-106.

Preston, George Nelson. "Techniques and Style in Akan Commemorative Terra Cottas," in *The Ancient Treasures of Mali and Ghana*. New York: The African-American Institute, 1981.

Simmons, Donald C. "The Depiction of Gangosa on Efik-Ibibio Masks," *Man*, 57 (1957): 17-20.

Thompson, Robert Farris. "Grand Detroit N'kondi," *Bulletin of the Detroit Institute of Arts*, 56, no. 4 (1978): 206-221.

Vander Hayden, Marsha. "The Epa Mask and Ceremony," *African Arts*, 10, no. 2 (1977): 14-21, 91.

Vogel, Susan M. "People of Wood: Baule Figure Sculpture," *Art Journal*, 33, no. 1 (1973): 23-26.

Wescott, Joan. "The Sculpture and Myths of Eshu-Elegba, The Yoruba Trickster," *Africa*, 32, no. 4 (1962): 336-53.

Wescott, Joan, and Peter Morton-Williams. "The Symbolism and Ritual Context of the Yoruba Laba Shango," *Journal of the Royal Anthropological Institute*, 92 (1962): 23-37.